The Christian Healthcare Leader

The Christian Healthcare Leader is a faith-centered, practical guide designed to equip current and aspiring leaders in healthcare to lead with wisdom, courage, and spiritual discernment.

As burnout, moral complexity, and institutional strain rise across the healthcare system, many leaders are seeking guidance not only on how to manage their organizations but also on how to lead in a way that reflects their deepest beliefs. This book offers 50 concise, actionable lessons that connect the demands of healthcare leadership with timeless Scriptural wisdom. Each lesson follows a structured approach: Leadership Principle → Biblical Insight → Practical Application, providing readers tools to lead with faith, courage, and clarity.

Unlike other leadership texts, this book focuses on both Christian principles and healthcare realities. Lessons draw on Scripture through key passages and stories, real-world healthcare leadership experience, and practical steps for integration into daily practice.

The Christian Healthcare Leader

50 Lessons in Faith, Courage, and Calling

Matthew Bogner

Routledge
Taylor & Francis Group
A PRODUCTIVITY PRESS BOOK

Designed cover image: Shutterstock

First published 2027
by Routledge
605 Third Avenue, New York, NY 10158

and by Routledge
4 Park Square, Milton Park, Abingdon, Oxon, OX14 4RN

Routledge is an imprint of the Taylor & Francis Group, an informa business

ISBN: 9781041294856 (hbk)
ISBN: 9781041294849 (pbk)
ISBN: 9781003769781 (ebk)

DOI: 10.4324/9781003769781

Typeset in Garamond
by Newgen Publishing UK

Contents

Introduction

When I first considered writing a book on Christian healthcare leadership, I reflected on my own journey as both a leader and a follower of Christ. I thought about how I had grown over the years and how deeply I relied on God's presence, guidance, and strength through it all.

Yet when it came time to begin writing, I struggled. I wasn't sure I had the right words or even the ability to write them. Could I really capture the weight and responsibility of this calling? Could I offer something meaningful to others walking this same path?

I remember praying: "Lord, if I'm not the one to write this book, then please send someone who can. Because this message is desperately needed by so many who are striving to be faithful, effective leaders."

I could feel how good it could be and was unsure of my ability to bring it to life. But in time, I found the courage to begin, and this book was born. I offer it to you with humility and hope. It may not be perfect, but it is sincere.

My prayer is that you find encouragement, wisdom, and perhaps a renewed sense of calling in these pages. I know how difficult this work can be and how deeply it affects those who are called to lead in it. Unless you've stood in the shoes of a healthcare leader, it's hard to truly understand the burden and the blessing of the role. But you are not alone. God is with you. And I pray that this book reminds you of that truth.

Blessings and peace,
Matthew

I

FOUNDATIONS OF FAITHFUL LEADERSHIP

Lesson 1

Redefine Success

Given the realities of today's healthcare system, it's time for Christian healthcare leaders to redefine what success truly means. This begins with shifting our mindset from career advancement to faithful stewardship. It also involves recognizing that traditional metrics such as clinical outcomes, financial performance, and satisfaction scores are important, but not always sufficient to measure what truly matters.

Excellence and high standards remain essential, but we must also recognize that quiet, faithful service holds profound value. It matters deeply to the people we lead and to those we care for. Often, the most meaningful impact isn't found in reports or ratings. It is found in small acts of compassion, integrity, and kindness that reflect God's love in tangible ways.

When Faith and Metrics Collide

One of the deepest tensions that Christian leaders face is the pull between institutional definitions of success and their spiritual calling. In healthcare, success is often equated with efficiency, profitability, and performance. But the call of Christ urges us to weigh those goals against compassion, justice, and human dignity.

Consider a leader praised for cutting services or staff to stabilize finances. The decision may be necessary, but the human and moral cost is real. How do we define success in those moments?

This is where discernment becomes essential. We're not called to abandon stewardship or responsibility. We are called to pursue those goals

DOI: 10.4324/9781003769781-2

without losing sight of our deeper mission: to love, to serve, and to stand with those who have little voice or influence.

Anchored by the Word

In moments of tension, when institutional expectations clash with the call to serve, Scripture offers clarity, comfort, and direction.

> Do nothing out of selfish ambition or vain conceit. Rather, in humility value others above yourselves.
>
> Philippians 2:3–7 (NIV)

This guidance reminds us that leadership is not about status, recognition, or personal ambition. Instead, we are called to support others, serve faithfully, and reflect the heart of Christ in every decision we make. True leadership is often quiet, unseen, and sacrificial. Yet it carries eternal significance.

> The Lord does not look at the things people look at. People look at the outward appearance, but the Lord looks at the heart.
>
> 1 Samuel 16:7 (NIV)

This verse reassures us that even when our efforts go unnoticed by others, God sees the intentions behind our actions. It also reminds us that faithfulness, integrity, and compassion matter more than metrics, reports, or accolades. Leadership, at its deepest level, is measured by the love, care, and commitment we bring to those we serve.

Serving Quietly, Leading Faithfully

Faithful leadership often happens away from the spotlight. It may look like a department head who listens more than they speak, who lifts up the voices of their team, and who seeks wisdom rather than control. Or an executive who shields staff members even when budgets are tight. Or someone who advocates persistently, without recognition, for those who are often overlooked.

It can also look like a leader who encourages staff members to form genuine relationships with those they care for. This means giving

permission to slow down and treat people with dignity rather than as tasks on a checklist. It's about helping them feel truly seen and heard at the deepest level.

These choices build trust and nurture a culture where people feel valued. They are not flashy, but they are powerful. This too is success. Not the kind defined by key performance indicators, but the kind that changes lives and honors God.

The Gift of Presence

When I was a nursing home administrator, I became close with one of our residents. She was the longtime companion of a man I knew through a local community organization. Over time, both of them became close friends of mine. Despite her health challenges, she was lively, vivacious, and unfailingly kind. She made a point of stopping by my office every day to see how I was doing and to chat. During these conversations, she also advocated for other residents, and we discussed the cultural changes I was leading.

Our conversations became a bright spot for me each day in a challenging job. I came to rely on her encouragement, her humor, and her friendship. Then one day, her companion passed away. Not long after, her health declined as well, and she was hospitalized. When I heard how serious it was, I went to see her to say goodbye.

I expected to find her alone, but a young relative was there. He appeared barely old enough to drive, and grief weighed heavily on him. He looked lost and unsure what to do, staring into the space beside her bed. She was barely conscious and struggling to breathe. I didn't know what to do or say, and I couldn't say goodbye the way I had planned because she couldn't hear me. I found myself at a loss for words with the family member she so clearly loved.

So, I asked him if he minded if I said a prayer for her. At this, he looked up as if seeing me for the first time and said with relief, "Yes… please." I did my best in that moment. It was not my most eloquent prayer, but it was sincere. I prayed for her, and I prayed for him too. Then we shared a few more words, and I left. That was it.

I had not thought about that memory for years, but it came to mind because those are the moments that truly matter. I am grateful that he did not have to be there by himself. I am grateful I had the opportunity to be with him for a moment during that difficult time. More than anything, I am grateful I invited God into that space so we could feel His presence together. Moments like these remind us that leadership is not only measured by metrics, but by the presence, care, and faithfulness we bring to those around us.

A Call to Redefine Success

As Christian leaders, we are called to a broader and deeper definition of success. In a system marked by complexity and scarcity, we cannot afford to lose sight of our calling: to lead with courage, to serve with grace, and to trust that even small acts of goodness ripple with eternal significance. God does not measure success by numbers or recognition. He looks for faithfulness, delights in mercy, and cherishes those who lead with love, especially when no one is watching. Let us redefine success. Not by what we achieve, but by how we live, how we lead, and how faithfully we reflect the heart of Christ.

Action Step 1: Audit Your Success Metrics

Review the performance indicators you or your team currently use to measure success. Ask: *What values are being rewarded? What might be missing?* Add one non-traditional measure (e.g., staff well-being, ethical consideration, or patient dignity) to your next leadership discussion.

Action Step 2: Champion One Quiet Leader This Week

Identify a colleague who models humility, compassion, or quiet service. Acknowledge their contribution publicly or privately as a way of honoring unseen faithfulness.

Action Step 3: Practice Listening Before Deciding

In your next decision-making process, commit to listening longer to staff, patients, or colleagues, before acting. Let discernment shape your leadership more than efficiency alone.

Action Step 4: Choose One Faithful Act Over Visible Results

Take one small action this week that reflects Christ's love. Especially one no one will see or praise. Let it be enough that God sees it.

Reflection and Journal Prompts

1. How have I been defining success lately? Reflect on whether your recent decisions and motivations align more with performance metrics or with faithfulness to Christ's example.
2. Who shaped my view of leadership? Think about the people or systems that influenced your leadership style. What would it look like to reshape that view through the lens of servant leadership?
3. Where is the tension in my leadership right now? Identify a current situation where your values conflict with institutional expectations. Ask God for clarity, courage, and compassion in that space.
4. Am I content with being unseen? Sit with the question: *Would I still make this choice if no one noticed but God?* Write honestly about your comfort or discomfort with hidden faithfulness.

Lesson 2

Know Who You Are Before You Lead

The best leaders know who they are, including their values, strengths, and limitations. This kind of self-awareness requires honest reflection, which can sometimes be uncomfortable. Yet it leads to authenticity and confidence, enabling leaders to bring out the best in themselves and others. It also equips them to withstand external pressures and criticism.

For Christian leaders, self-awareness goes even deeper. It means grounding our identity in something eternal, as beloved children of God and followers of Jesus Christ. This foundation allows us to lead from a spiritual identity rather than a title or role. When we understand who we are in Christ, we no longer need to prove ourselves through achievement or comparison. Our worth is already settled. From that place of security, we can lead with humility and courage, serving others rather than seeking validation. As Paul reminds us,

> For we are God's handiwork, created in Christ Jesus to do good works, which God prepared in advance for us to do.
>
> *Ephesians 2:10 (NIV)*

Know Your Strengths

Before you can lead effectively, you must understand your strengths. For example, I am guided by a clear set of beliefs that shape my decisions,

DOI: 10.4324/9781003769781-3

anchor my purpose, and influence how I lead. I find joy in developing others, helping them recognize their potential and grow into their best selves. My drive pushes me to set meaningful goals and follow through with persistence. I thrive on communication, connecting with others, sharing ideas clearly, and inspiring collaboration. My love of learning keeps me curious, open, and committed to growth.

Consider what energizes you, which tasks feel natural, and the contributions others seek from you. Feedback from colleagues, mentors, or supervisors can provide valuable insight. In addition, structured assessments can help clarify your gifts.

Know Your Limitations

Equally important is recognizing your limitations. This can feel uncomfortable but is essential for growth. Honest feedback is key, even though some may hesitate to offer it. Feedback can reveal gaps in skills, knowledge, or interpersonal abilities. Some areas can be improved with effort, while others may require ongoing support. This is natural. No one can excel at everything.

For example, I thrive in strategy, creativity, and forward motion, but I rely on others for administrative or back-end tasks. I can also be impatient at times. Recognizing these limitations has been freeing and allows me to focus my energy where it has the greatest impact.

Know Your Values

Your values act as a compass, guiding your decisions, interactions, and responses to challenges. They define what matters most, shape priorities, and influence how you lead. Reflection and prayer help clarify these principles, which serve as both a spiritual and professional anchor.

Leaders who are clear about their values act with integrity, make consistent decisions, and inspire trust. Without this foundation, even capable leaders can drift, lose focus, or struggle to align actions with their mission. Knowing your values enables you to serve your team, patients, and organization with authenticity and purpose.

Know Your Identity in Christ

For Christian healthcare leaders, leadership is grounded in a relationship with Jesus Christ. Our decisions, priorities, and interactions flow from who we are in Him, not merely from skills or strategies. This identity shapes how we respond to challenges, care for patients, and serve our teams with intentionality, humility, and compassion.

Leading from Christ means acting with integrity under pressure, nurturing others, and maintaining perspective in difficult situations. It is about serving others as an expression of God's love and reflecting His character in every interaction. This foundation allows leaders to lead faithfully, serve meaningfully, and remain rooted in their calling, regardless of circumstances.

Knowing Who You Are Is a Lifelong Endeavor

Understanding yourself is an ongoing journey guided by God as He shapes your path. As you walk with Him, cultivate habits that nurture self-awareness. Seek feedback, talk to God in prayer, revisit your values regularly, and spend time in honest reflection. These practices help you stay attuned to your strengths, limitations, and priorities.

By embracing this journey, you position yourself to lead with faithfulness and intention. Self-awareness enables you to serve others in ways that honor both God and the people entrusted to your care. It also helps you make decisions with clarity, act with integrity, and stay aligned with your calling.

Action Step 1: Reflect on What Energizes You

Set aside time this week to identify activities, tasks, or interactions that bring you energy and joy. These often indicate your natural strengths and areas where God may be calling you to lead.

Action Step 2: Seek Honest Feedback

Invite a trusted colleague, mentor, or friend to share one strength they see in you and one area for growth. Receive their feedback with humility and gratitude, using it as a tool for greater self-awareness.

Action Step 3: Clarify Your Core Values

Write down your top three to five guiding values. Consider how these align with your daily decisions and leadership choices. Ask God to help you lead in ways that reflect these values consistently.

Action Step 4: Reaffirm Your Identity in Christ

Spend time in prayer or Scripture, reflecting on what it means to lead from an identity in Christ. Let this truth ground your confidence, direction, and purpose as a leader.

Journal and Reflection Prompts

1. When in your work do you feel most alive and effective? What does that reveal about the strengths God has placed within you?
2. Think of a time when someone gave you constructive feedback that was hard to hear but ultimately helped you grow. What did you learn about yourself through that experience?
3. What are the values that guide your leadership decisions? Where do you see alignment or tension between your stated values and your daily actions?
4. How does knowing your identity in Christ shape the way you lead? In what areas do you need to trust God more fully to lead through you rather than relying on your own strength?

Lesson 3

Clarify Your Calling

Healthcare is more than a profession. It is a vocation rooted in God's purpose. Many in healthcare say they have been called to this work. But what does that truly mean?

Career vs. Calling

We must first distinguish between a career and a calling. A career is something you choose. A calling is something you receive. A career may focus on achievement, advancement, or success, while a calling centers on faithfulness, service, and purpose. Those who sense a calling recognize that they are in this field for a reason and that their work carries meaning beyond personal ambition or circumstance.

Calling is a foundational theme of Christian leadership. In healthcare, it serves as an anchor amid burnout, bureaucracy, and relentless performance pressure. When success metrics fall short or recognition fades, a sense of calling sustains you. It redefines motivation, strengthens endurance, and renews joy in the work God has entrusted to you.

The Nature of Calling

Some people are called to a vocation as a lifelong endeavor. Others are called to a role or field for a particular season. This distinction is

DOI: 10.4324/9781003769781-4

important, especially in healthcare, where stress and turnover are high. Many leaders begin new roles with energy and vision, only to find the pace and pressure unsustainable. While the level of strain varies across roles, the challenges of today's healthcare environment are significant for everyone.

Recognizing this reality helps us approach our work with both commitment and humility. The key is to honor your calling while protecting your mental, emotional, and physical health. A healthy perspective says: *While I am in this position, I will do my best to live out my calling through Christlike values and leadership. I will seek God's support and direction. I will rely on others whom God has placed alongside me. I will remain humble and open to where He may lead next.*

When we hold our calling with this kind of faithfulness, firm in purpose yet flexible in season, we find freedom. God's calling is not limited to one job or title. It is an ongoing invitation to serve, grow, and reflect His love wherever we are placed.

Hearing God Through Prayer

Recognizing God's direction begins with a personal relationship with Him. How often do you go to God in prayer? How open are you about your fears, doubts, and needs? Have you invited Him into your life? Do you speak with Him as with a friend, honestly, continually, and with trust? Do you admit your shortcomings and ask for strength, guidance, and direction?

In my own walk with God, I have sought this kind of relationship. When I pray, it is not transactional. It is deeply personal and transformational. I have invited God into my life, asked Him to go before me, and trusted that He is always with me. I have offered myself to His plans, knowing they are better than my own. I believe that God will enter your life and guide your path if you simply ask Him. Remember this promise:

> Ask and it will be given to you; seek and you will find; knock and the door will be opened to you. For everyone who asks receives; the one who seeks finds; and to the one who knocks, the door will be opened.
>
> Matthew 7:7–8 (NIV)

Hearing God Through Scripture

God also speaks to us through Scripture, His living Word, which continually reveals truth, direction, and encouragement. Consider starting with the Gospels and then moving through the rest of the New Testament. It doesn't have to be much. Start small. The key is developing a daily habit of reflection. Even fifteen minutes in the evening can be meaningful. As you read, reflect on how each passage connects to your leadership, your relationships, and the way you live out your calling in daily life.

Hearing God Through People

In addition, God may use others to confirm, challenge, or clarify our sense of direction. Sometimes, others notice gifts or qualities in us before we do. A friend, colleague, or mentor might say, "You're really good at this" or "You have a gift." In healthcare, this could look like a mentor affirming your readiness for a new challenge or a team member recognizing that your leadership reflects Christlike compassion. Wise counsel from experienced individuals can also help us discern whether our sense of calling aligns with God's plan. Trusted mentors and friends provide accountability, helping ensure that our calling remains grounded in biblical values rather than driven by ambition, fear, or pride. As we are reminded in Proverbs:

> For lack of guidance a nation falls, but victory is won through many advisers.
>
> Proverbs 11:14 (NIV)

Hearing God Through Circumstances

God also guides us through the open and closed doors of life, including the events, opportunities, and challenges we encounter.

- Sometimes a closed door, such as a job loss, denied opportunity, or failed project, allows God to redirect us toward a place where our gifts and calling will flourish.

- Sometimes an open door, such as a new opportunity, timely connection, or need that stirs our heart, is God inviting us to step forward in faith.
- In both cases, the question is not "Why did this happen?" but "Lord, what are You teaching me through this?"

One prayer I have prayed for years is this: Lord, please keep the wrong doors closed and the right ones open. It sounds simple, but it is powerful. It brings peace, even when things do not go as planned, because I know God's path is better than my own.

> And we know that in all things God works for the good of those who love him, who have been called according to his purpose.
>
> Romans 8:28 (NIV)

Living Out Your Calling

Discovering your calling is only the beginning. Living it out is a daily act of faith and obedience. As you do this:

- **Stay Connected to God.** Make prayer, Scripture, and reflection part of your daily rhythm. Let His voice shape your decisions more than ambition or pressure.
- **Seek Wisdom and Support.** Surround yourself with mentors, colleagues, and friends who can affirm, guide, and challenge you.
- **Respond to Circumstances with Faith.** Pay attention to the open and closed doors in your life, trusting that God is shaping your path, even through setbacks and delays.
- **Serve with Purpose.** Let your calling infuse everything you do, from quiet acts of kindness to major decisions. Your work is part of a larger story in God's hands.

Living out your calling does not require perfection or certainty. It requires faithfulness, humility, and courage to step into the work God has placed before you in this moment. As you do, you'll find meaning that transcends metrics, recognition, or temporary success.

Stand firm, knowing that God will provide the strength and guidance you need. Remember that callings can change, and that's okay. Protect your mental, emotional, and physical well-being. You cannot give what you do not have. Cultivate peace, energy, and joy so that you can serve others with love, patience, and compassion. Finally, stay rooted in a community of believers devoted to these shared values, who will walk with you, encourage you, and remind you of God's faithfulness. In that community, your calling will not only be sustained but strengthened.

Action Step 1: Deepen Your Relationship with God

Prioritize daily prayer, Scripture reading, and reflection. Invite God's guidance into your decisions and work.

Action Step 2: Seek Wisdom and Accountability

Surround yourself with mentors, colleagues, and friends who can affirm, guide, and challenge you in alignment with God's purpose.

Action Step 3: Trust God Through Circumstances

Pay attention to open and closed doors in life. Ask what God is teaching you in each situation and step forward in faith.

Action Step 4: Serve with Purpose and Care

Let your calling guide your actions, prioritizing love, patience, and compassion. Protect your well-being so that you can give your best to others.

Reflection and Journal Prompts

1. Reflect on a moment when you felt most aligned with your calling. What were you doing, and what does that reveal about your purpose?

2. Think about a recent challenge or "closed door" in your work. How might God have been redirecting you? What lessons or insights can you take from it?
3. Consider the people who have shaped your professional and spiritual growth. How have mentors, colleagues, or friends helped clarify or confirm your calling?
4. Examine a typical week in your life. Which actions or decisions are fully aligned with your calling, and which might need adjustment to reflect God's purpose more clearly?

Lesson 4

Lead Faithfully in Secular Spaces

Healthcare is a broad field with many types of organizations. Some Christian leaders serve in faith-based settings, where they can openly discuss their beliefs and live out their values. Others serve in secular settings, where expressing faith calls for discernment, wisdom, and sensitivity.

This lesson is especially for leaders serving in secular spaces, and I want to share my perspective on the differences between faith-based and secular settings. In some cases, cultural differences are clear. In others, they are subtle or harder to detect. The experience often depends on the organization as well as the national, regional, and local leaders in place. I worked in one faith-based system where I had a very positive experience, while another proved extremely challenging. The differences came down to organizational structure, policies, decision-making processes, and how people were treated in daily interactions.

The truth is, not every faith-based organization is ideal, and not every secular organization is flawed. Both types of healthcare organizations attract people who are called to serve and help others. Ultimately, culture is shaped by local leaders, and the most important leader for any of us is our direct supervisor. Wherever we are called to serve, we each have the opportunity to reflect the heart of Christ. While some environments may make this easier than others, faithful leadership is always possible when we lead with humility, integrity, and a sincere desire to serve those entrusted to our care.

 DOI: 10.4324/9781003769781-5

Principles for Faithful Leadership in Secular Spaces

If you serve in a secular healthcare setting, the following principles can support you in leading faithfully.

- **Lead with Christlike character, not just Christian language**.
Consider someone who frequently talks about their faith, but whose behavior is unkind, arrogant, or abrasive. Their words, rather than drawing others closer, often push people away. Too often, the focus seems to be on being religious rather than cultivating genuine faith, humility, and a personal relationship with Jesus Christ. In contrast, a leader with a deep relationship with Christ does not feel the need to constantly broadcast their beliefs. Their actions naturally reflect their faith, demonstrating integrity, compassion, and humility. When appropriate, they share their faith thoughtfully and supportively, in ways that honor God and respect others. This approach requires discernment, confidence in your relationship with God, and a humble recognition that influence comes more from how we live than from what we say.
- **Let your actions speak before your words**.
Even in settings where speaking about your faith is limited, your actions always communicate your values. Actions often open doors for conversations that words alone never could. Examples include showing empathy to difficult patients or colleagues, taking responsibility rather than shifting blame, advocating for justice and equity, and treating every person with kindness, dignity, and respect.
- **Practice wisdom and discernment**.
Faithful leadership is not about pushing your beliefs on others. It is about knowing when and how to express them in ways that honor Christ while respecting the workplace. This involves understanding organizational culture, reading relational cues, responding with grace rather than reacting, recognizing when silence is wise, and navigating policies around religious expression.
- **Create a culture of care and human dignity**.
While you may not be able to establish explicitly Christian systems, you can implement processes that reflect Christ's compassion and commitment to justice. Examples include building supportive team cultures, practicing ethical decision-making, prioritizing

patient-centered care, protecting vulnerable populations, and encouraging fairness and transparency.

- **Influence through servant leadership**.
Regardless of your authority level, you can lead by serving others. Servant leadership is rooted in Christian values and widely respected in secular healthcare. This involves putting others' needs above your own, empowering your team, listening actively, helping others succeed, and modeling calm and steady leadership in times of crisis.
- **Stay rooted in your faith outside the workplace**.
Your ability to lead faithfully inside the workplace depends on how grounded you are outside of it. Ways to stay rooted include daily prayer and reflection on Scripture, participating in a supportive Christian community, observing Sabbath and intentional rest, and maintaining spiritual disciplines such as regular personal worship. By nurturing your relationship with God consistently, you build the strength, clarity, and humility needed to lead effectively in any setting.
- **Cultivate courage and conviction**.
There will be moments when faithfulness requires courage, such as speaking up, making a difficult decision, or standing alone. Examples include navigating ethical dilemmas, resisting pressure to compromise your values, responding to criticism or misunderstanding, and protecting staff or patients from harmful practices. By leaning on your convictions and trusting God's guidance, you can lead with integrity even in challenging circumstances.
- **Trust God with the results**.
Faithful leadership does not guarantee easy outcomes, but God is honored by your obedience, not by your ability to control results. Ways to cultivate this principle include surrendering outcomes to God, recognizing that influence is often slow and unseen, and understanding that faithfulness itself is the true measure of success in God's eyes.

Putting Faithful Leadership into Practice

Concrete examples of how these principles can be lived out in healthcare organizations include:

- Leading meetings with humility
- Handling difficult conversations with grace and discernment

- Advocating for fairness, patient-centered care, or staff well-being
- Modeling servant leadership in small actions, such as checking in on a team member, taking responsibility, or supporting someone who is struggling
- Maintaining spiritual disciplines outside work to stay grounded for leadership decisions

Difficult conversations occur regularly in healthcare leadership. These may involve leadership team members, frontline staff, patients, or family members, and often arise from grievances or emotionally charged situations. Absorbing feedback while maintaining calm, composure, and grace is challenging but one of the most impactful ways to lead in a Christlike manner.

In addition, staff well-being is critically important, given the high levels of stress and turnover among frontline staff, managers, and senior leaders. Part of keeping good people in these positions is prioritizing their holistic health. While resource constraints can make this feel like an intractable problem, Christian leaders distinguish themselves by making staff well-being a priority in both words and actions. This requires a mindset shift: the health of the workforce is as important as the health of those they serve.

Servant leadership is especially evident in regular check-ins and support for those who are struggling. Focus on the whole person, not just performance. Ask how they are coping personally and how work is affecting them. Only after addressing these deeper concerns can leaders effectively discuss performance.

Supporting staff may involve addressing emotional and mental fatigue caused by work overload, the stressful nature of caregiving, long hours, or difficulty disengaging from work at home. It may also result from poorly planned role transitions or training. With consolidation of positions, many staff are now asked to perform the work of two or three people, a clearly unsustainable situation. Leaders must recognize and address these systemic challenges while validating the feelings of staff. Struggle is not a personal flaw or weakness. It is a natural response to working in an imperfect system.

Maintaining spiritual disciplines is equally critical. A personal relationship with Jesus Christ is the foundation for faithful leadership. Invite Him into your work and lean on Him for guidance, wisdom, and strength. There are no perfect solutions to the challenges of healthcare, and outcomes may not always meet expectations. But what matters most is leading faithfully and depending on God for the results. By grounding yourself spiritually, you can serve with resilience, wisdom, and Christlike love, even in the most challenging secular settings.

While the environments and systems may be imperfect, your influence as a Christian leader matters. This includes your character, your actions, and your commitment to serving others. By practicing the principles discussed above, you can impact the people and organizations around you for good.

Remember, faithful leadership is a journey, not a destination. Even small, consistent acts can reflect Christ's heart in powerful ways. Lead with confidence, humility, and dependence on God, knowing that He honors your faithfulness, even when outcomes are uncertain.

Action Step 1: Reflect Daily on Your Leadership

Take 10–15 minutes each day to evaluate your actions and decisions. Ask yourself: *Am I leading with Christlike character? Are my words and actions reflecting integrity, humility, and compassion?* Use journaling or prayer to identify areas for growth and to stay grounded in your faith.

Action Step 2: Prioritize Staff Well-Being

Implement at least one intentional action each week to support your team's holistic health. This could include personal check-ins, advocating for fair workload distribution, encouraging rest and boundaries, or connecting staff to resources for mental and emotional support.

Action Step 3: Practice Servant Leadership in Tangible Ways

Identify one opportunity each week to serve others in your organization, whether it's mentoring a colleague, helping a struggling team member, or taking responsibility for a challenge rather than assigning blame. Focus on actions that demonstrate care and model Christlike service.

Action Step 4: Trust God with Outcomes

After making decisions or taking action, intentionally surrender the results to God. Reflect on areas where outcomes are beyond your control and commit them in prayer. Remember that faithfulness, not perfection, is the measure of success in God's eyes.

Reflection and Journal Prompts

1. Reflect on a recent leadership decision or interaction. Did your words and actions reflect Christlike character? Where could you have demonstrated more integrity, humility, or compassion?
2. Think about a challenging conversation you've had or anticipate having in your workplace. How can you approach it with wisdom, grace, and discernment, honoring both Christ and the people involved?
3. Journal about ways you are currently supporting the well-being of your team. Are there opportunities to serve them more fully, both personally and professionally, in alignment with your Christian values?
4. Consider a recent situation where the outcome was beyond your control. How did you respond? How might you better surrender results to God in future situations, while still leading faithfully and making wise decisions?

Lesson 5

Align Ambition with God's Will

As Christian healthcare leaders, we are called to surrender personal ambition to God's greater purpose. Sometimes ambition takes the form of a desire for success, achievement, or recognition. It may also include aspirations for advancement, wealth, or personal gain. These feelings are natural, and a healthy measure of ambition can be useful. But when ambition becomes the driving force of our lives, it must be tempered and placed behind our beliefs, values, and purpose.

Ambition is not always about achievement. Sometimes it reflects a longing for a specific path we hope our lives will follow. In those moments, surrendering to God's plans can be especially difficult, particularly when the doors we expected to open remain firmly closed.

A Journey of Surrendered Ambition

In my own life, I have wrestled with both forms of ambition: personal achievement and the desire for a particular path I hoped God would affirm. As a young professional, I was driven, goal-oriented, and eager to succeed. Yet I also longed for deeper meaning, purpose, and alignment with God's will. Over time, through my growing relationship with God and daily conversations with Him, my focus began to shift. Achievement mattered less. Listening, discerning, and living out my values mattered more.

DOI: 10.4324/9781003769781-6

From a young age, I prayed that God would allow me to be part of something bigger than myself. I felt called to ordained ministry and told God I would go wherever He led. It was a sincere prayer, but one that required great trust, especially when the path unfolded differently than I expected.

Instead of entering pastoral ministry, I pursued degrees in psychology, public health, and health administration. My career took me into mental health, long-term care, senior living, and health system administration. These roles were meaningful, at times deeply fulfilling, and at other times heavy with responsibility. Anyone who has led in healthcare understands the weight that comes with serving vulnerable people and guiding complex organizations.

After serving as a nonprofit healthcare leader, I completed my doctorate and arrived at a crossroads. I felt drawn to teaching in higher education, yet the call to pastoral ministry resurfaced with equal force. In my denomination, pursuing ordination involves a lengthy discernment process in which both the candidate and the church must confirm the call.

I entered the process twice. The first time, I reached the halfway point before realizing that the required itinerancy would be extremely difficult for my wife and children. It was painful and confusing. I felt called, yet the structure did not fit our family's needs. I stepped away and began teaching as a university professor in health administration.

Teaching fit me well. It aligned with my strengths in developing others, communication, and learning. I conducted research, published in scholarly journals, and found joy in shaping future leaders. Still, I struggled to release my early calling to serve the church in an ordained pastoral role.

When the call persisted, I returned to the ordination process and completed the discernment requirements. I was certified as a candidate for ministry, yet the same barriers remained. Once again, I stepped back.

In the years that followed, God revealed a path I had not imagined. Through writing, teaching, and mentoring, I pursued both aspects of my calling: forming values-based leaders and engaging in meaningful ministry beyond a formal pastoral role. It took time, wrestling, and surrender, but I came to see that God was shaping a different form of ministry for me in that season. As I look ahead, I trust that God will continue to weave together my gifts, my experiences, and the desires He placed in my heart long ago.

Holding Ambition with Open Hands

As you reflect on your own ambition, I hope this offers reassurance and perspective. Even when we cannot see the full path ahead, God already knows it. When we invite Him to go before us and tell Him we are open to His plans, we learn to surrender both our ambition and the burden that comes with it. In doing so, we release anxiety and trust Him more fully, allowing God to guide us into vocational work that aligns with our deepest identity and His purpose in the world.

I also want to offer you words of hope. Sometimes an unanswered prayer isn't a "no." Sometimes God is simply saying, "not yet." It may be a matter of timing, preparation, or formation. A pastor once shared that perspective with me as I wrestled with my own calling to ordained ministry, and his words have stayed with me.

God knows the desires of your heart. When those desires are rooted in service, compassion, and a longing to participate in His work, you can trust that He has heard them. You can also trust Him to lead your path, wherever you are called to serve.

Action Step 1: Examine Your Ambition Honestly before God

Set aside time this week to prayerfully reflect on what drives you, including your goals, desires, motivations, and anxieties. Ask God to reveal where your ambition aligns with Him and where it may be rooted in pride, fear, or a desire for control.

Action Step 2: Identify One Area where You Need to Release Control

Consider a specific goal, opportunity, or expectation you are holding tightly. Practice surrender by praying, "God, this belongs to You. Lead me in Your timing and in Your way."

Action Step 3: Seek Wise Counsel and Spiritual Discernment

Invite a pastor, mentor, or trusted Christian colleague to speak into your sense of calling or career direction. Listen with openness, believing that God often guides us through the wisdom of others.

Action Step 4: Take One Step that Aligns Your Work with God's Purpose

Choose a practical action such as serving a colleague, strengthening a value-driven practice, or integrating prayer into your leadership decisions that moves you toward living out your calling more fully and faithfully in your current role.

Reflection and Journal Prompts

1. Where do you see ambition in your life, and where might ambition be overshadowing trust in God? Reflect on how each type of ambition shows up in your leadership, career decisions, or long-term hopes.
2. What closed door or delayed "yes" in your life has been the hardest to accept? Write about how it affected you emotionally and spiritually, and how you sense God may have been shaping you through it.
3. When have you most clearly felt God aligning your vocation with your gifts, values, and identity? Describe that moment or season. What does it reveal about how God guides you?
4. What desire of your heart do you need to place before God with open hands? Journal a prayer of surrender, expressing your willingness to follow God's timing, direction, and purpose.

Lesson 6

Lead with Love

One of the most essential foundations of Christian leadership is the call to lead with love. Though it may sound simple, especially within the complexity of today's healthcare system, it provides a powerful counterbalance to the many challenges leaders face. Leading with love provides a guiding lens for decision making, especially in ethically complicated situations. At its core, it invites leaders to pause and ask: *Does this choice reflect the love of God at work in me and through me?*

The Character of Love in Action

This principle becomes even more powerful when viewed through the lens of Paul's teaching on the character of love:

> Love is patient, love is kind. It does not envy, it does not boast, it is not proud. It does not dishonor others, it is not self-seeking, it is not easily angered, it keeps no record of wrongs. Love does not delight in evil but rejoices with the truth. It always protects, always trusts, always hopes, always perseveres. Love never fails.
>
> 1 Corinthians 13:4–8 (NIV)

This passage is particularly helpful for leaders because "love" can mean many things to many people. Here, we receive concrete guidance. It allows leaders to ask whether their leadership and decisions are grounded in

DOI: 10.4324/9781003769781-7

patience, kindness, truth, protection, trust, hope, and perseverance. At the same time, it invites reflection on whether actions are motivated by pride, anger, resentment, selfish ambition, or a desire to harm or dishonor others. Using this lens, leaders can measure decisions and behaviors against a timeless standard of love that endures even in difficult situations.

Leading with Love in the Workplace

When applied to healthcare, leading with love takes on practical, visible forms. Here are several ways it can be lived out:

- **Listening fully before responding.** Giving someone your undivided attention communicates dignity and respect, even when time is short.
- **Treating staff with patience during high-stress situations.** Choosing calm, steady leadership when emotions run high models the patience described in Scripture.
- **Offering kindness in everyday interactions.** Small gestures, such as checking in on a struggling employee or affirming someone's hard work, create a culture of care.
- **Assuming the best in others.** Rather than jumping to conclusions or blaming, leaders who operate from trust strengthen team relationships.
- **Addressing conflict without anger or defensiveness.** Love-driven leaders confront issues directly but with gentleness and humility.
- **Avoiding favoritism or comparison.** Showing fairness and honoring each person's contributions demonstrates respect for others.
- **Not keeping grudges.** Leaders who do not hold past mistakes against people create space for growth, restoration, and second chances.
- **Protecting the dignity of team members.** This includes speaking up when staff are treated unfairly, advocating for safe workloads, and preventing harmful gossip.
- **Rejoicing in truth.** Recognizing honesty, transparency, ethical decision-making, and integrity reinforces a culture built on truth.
- **Persevering through difficulty with hope.** Love empowers leaders to remain steady and hopeful when facing organizational challenges, staffing shortages, or ethical dilemmas.

Leading with Love Also Means Self-Love

In addition to treating others with love, it is essential to extend that same love toward yourself. Faith-driven leaders are often hard on themselves, whether for mistakes, missed opportunities, or imperfect outcomes. Yet Scripture never calls us to perfection in every moment. No one can rise to that standard.

Instead, we are invited to begin each day with courage, returning with a renewed sense of commitment. It can be helpful to think of each day as a gift. After all, none of us know how many we have left. The key is to view each day as an opportunity to enjoy the gifts God has given us and to bless others through our interactions.

When it comes to outcomes, leaders can be especially unforgiving toward themselves. The higher a leader rises, the more accountability they carry. To some extent, this is appropriate, but in healthcare many performance outcomes are shaped by factors beyond a leader's control. The truth is this: to forgive others, you must also learn to forgive yourself. It is difficult to hold yourself to an impossibly high standard while extending Christlike grace to others. When you love yourself, you are more able to love others. You cannot give what you do not possess inside.

It is also important to recognize that certain emotions can block our capacity to love. Anger, fear, resentment, and bitterness can quietly choke it out. These emotions are universal and deeply human, yet we still have a choice in how we respond to them, whether we cling to them or release them. Releasing them means allowing yourself to feel them fully, without shame, and then letting them go. Many tools can help with this process, but a combination of daily meditation and the spiritual practice of prayer is especially powerful.

Renewing the Mind

Mental reframing and pattern-breaking can also support self-love. Reframing allows a leader to interrupt unhealthy thoughts such as "I'm not good enough to fix the financial problems here", and replace them with healthier perspectives like, "I can lead faithfully, do my part, and trust God with what is beyond my control." Pattern-breaking goes a step further. It refers to intentionally disrupting automatic emotional or behavioral cycles that lead to discouragement, stress, or self-criticism. For example, if you habitually react to pressure with anxiety or self-blame, a pattern-breaking step might be to pause, take three slow breaths, step away for two minutes, or pray a short grounding prayer. These small, intentional interruptions weaken old patterns and create space for new, healthier responses. Over time, practices like these reshape the inner life, making room for grace, compassion, and a deeper experience of God's love. When leaders learn to lovingly steward their own minds and hearts, they become far better equipped to lead others with steadiness, clarity, and genuine love.

Reflecting God's Love for Us

For Christians, leading with love is possible because we first know what it means to be loved by God. Through the life, teachings, and sacrificial death of Jesus, the nature of God's love has been made unmistakably clear: patient, kind, forgiving, steadfast, and unfailing. When this truth moves from our minds to our hearts, it becomes far easier to reflect that same love toward others in our daily encounters.

Leading with love is not about perfection. It is about direction. It is the ongoing commitment to let God's love shape our thoughts, words, and decisions, especially in moments when it would be easier to react out of frustration, fear, or pride. As we grow in our awareness of God's love for us, we grow in our capacity to extend love to those we lead, those we serve, and those who depend on us.

Ultimately, love becomes both the standard and the source of Christian leadership. When leaders draw from the deep well of God's love, they bring compassion, clarity, courage, and hope into environments that genuinely need them. In this way, leading with love is not merely a strategy. It is a witness to the God who loved us first and continues to love us without fail.

Action Step 1: Pause and Reflect Before Decisions

Before making important choices, ask yourself: *Does this decision reflect the love of God working in me and through me?* Use Paul's description of love in 1 Corinthians 13 as a lens to evaluate whether your actions are patient, kind, truthful, protective, hopeful, and persevering.

Action Step 2: Practice Active, Compassionate Listening

Make it a daily practice to give undivided attention to those you lead. Listen not just to respond, but to understand and affirm the dignity of the person before you. This cultivates trust, patience, and kindness in your workplace.

Action Step 3: Engage in Self-Love and Self-Reflection

Set aside time each day to reflect on your own thoughts, emotions, and behaviors. Use techniques like mental reframing, pattern-breaking, meditation, and prayer to release anger, fear, resentment, or self-criticism. Remember that loving yourself enables you to lead others more effectively.

Action Step 4: Intentionally Demonstrate Love in Actions

Identify at least one practical way each day to model love in your leadership. This could include protecting a team member's dignity, affirming honest work, resolving conflict with humility, or showing patience in stressful situations. Over time, these consistent acts shape a culture of love and trust.

Reflection and Journal Prompts

1. Think about a recent decision you made as a leader. To what extent was it motivated by love—patience, kindness, truth, hope—or by pride, anger, or fear? How might you approach a similar situation differently in the future?
2. How do you currently treat yourself when you make mistakes or face challenges at work? What steps could you take to extend grace and compassion to yourself, just as you would to others?
3. Consider your daily interactions with your team. Are there moments where you could intentionally listen more fully, affirm others, or act with patience and kindness? List at least two specific actions you could take this week to lead with love.

4. Reflect on emotions such as anger, fear, resentment, or bitterness that may be affecting your leadership. What practices such as prayer, meditation, journaling, or pattern-breaking could help you acknowledge, release, and transform these emotions into constructive energy for leading with love?

Lesson 7

Care for Your Soul in the Storm

The best leaders intentionally care for their physical, mental, and spiritual health. They prioritize practices that support sustainable leadership, both for themselves and for their teams. In today's healthcare environment, burnout is common, but caring for your soul is still a choice.

That said, many leaders feel torn between doing the job well and protecting their own well-being. There is a pervasive expectation that leadership requires unrelenting hours, including days, nights, weekends, and holidays. It doesn't matter that hourly staff can fully disengage when they clock out. After all, leaders carry ultimate responsibility for organizational outcomes.

The result of this mindset is a lingering sense of guilt, fear, and pressure that pushes leaders into unsustainable patterns. But there is a better way. You may feel skeptical, and rightly so. Many argue there are not enough resources, including staffing, time, or money, to support healthier rhythms. Leadership roles have been consolidated in recent years as a result, requiring leaders to perform multiple roles simultaneously.

Even so, caring for your own well-being is not a luxury. It is a necessity. Small, intentional practices can create space for rest, reflection, and renewal, even in high-pressure environments. By setting boundaries, prioritizing personal health, and focusing on rhythms within your control, leaders not only protect themselves but also model sustainable practices for their teams.

DOI: 10.4324/9781003769781-8

Over time, these choices strengthen resilience, improve decision-making, and cultivate a culture that honors both patient care and the health of those who lead.

A More Hopeful Way Forward

It's understandable why you may feel skeptical about possible solutions. But the goal here isn't to fix the entire healthcare system. It is to help leaders faithfully navigate it. When framed this way, meaningful and realistic recommendations are possible. They don't require more staff, bigger budgets, or systemic overhauls. Instead, they focus on what leaders can control: rhythms, boundaries, culture, habits, and spiritual formation.

It is also important to recognize that culture and expectations vary significantly across healthcare settings. The hours and demands look different in clinics, hospitals, and skilled nursing facilities. While hospitals may be among the most challenging environments, there are still opportunities to support healthier leadership there as well.

The burden often falls hardest on clinical leaders, who face the dual pressure of leadership responsibilities and staffing shortages that push them to fill shifts on the floor. For this reason, prioritizing the well-being of these leaders is especially vital. With that said, let's explore some practical ways to protect your soul in the storm.

Set Sustainable Rhythms, Not Idealistic Ones

Leaders can control rhythms, even if they can't control workload. The following are small, soul-preserving practices that are realistic and practical. The important thing is to be consistent and start small, then increase them as your situation allows:

- Short daily rituals of stillness (2–5 minutes)
- A weekly Sabbath, one full day each week, from email and decision-making
- A monthly half-day for reflection and prayer
- One work-free night per week

Redefine What Healthy Leadership Looks Like

Changing your internal narrative creates permission to live differently. This is where you can help other leaders unlearn the "martyr model":

- Emphasize stewardship over self-sacrifice
- Teach that rest is part of leadership responsibility, not a reward
- Give language for teams to normalize boundaries (e.g., "for sustainability," "to model healthy leadership," "to reduce risk")
- Normalize boundaries in explicitly faith-based terms

Build Micro-Communities of Support

Soul care often collapses when leaders try to do it alone. Structure helps them succeed. Even in the busiest settings, leaders can cultivate:

- A spiritual mentor or prayer partner
- A small leadership peer group (15–20 minutes weekly)
- A single colleague who holds them accountable to rest
- A chaplain or pastor who checks in on them

Simplify and Automate Where Possible

Streamlining reduces the emotional and mental strain that leads to burnout. Practical approaches that reduce the weight of leadership include:

- Create standard decision pathways for common scenarios
- Delegate one category of decision each quarter
- Use templates and checklists to reduce cognitive load
- Conduct "stop doing" exercises to eliminate low-value tasks
- Develop or expand on-call rotation schedules among leaders

Integrate Spiritual Practices into Leadership

Soul care becomes a rhythm, not an appointment. Instead of adding more to your plate, integrate it into your workday:

- Begin meetings with a grounding moment or Scripture
- Practice breath prayer on the walk between units
- Make debriefings spiritual as well as clinical
- Turn difficult moments into opportunities to rely on God

Build a Culture That Encourages Healthy Limits

Cultural shifts start small but have ripple effects. Leaders can influence culture even if they cannot overhaul systems:

- Praise team members who model healthy boundaries
- Avoid glorifying overwork
- Set realistic email expectations (no response needed after hours)
- Have transparent conversations with executives about sustainable leadership practices

It Starts at the Top

Soul-healthy leadership always starts at the top. Senior leaders profoundly influence both the culture of an organization and the well-being of every member of the leadership team. Consider an organization that takes pride in having higher staffing levels for patients than others in the region. But there is a hidden cost. They only achieve this by cutting leadership positions, leaving the remaining leaders overwhelmed by crushing workloads, unrealistic expectations, and multiplied responsibilities. Leadership roles are consolidated to the point that sustainability becomes impossible. What is most concerning is that the organization recognizes this and still takes pride in it, saying, "We put patients first."

But what message does this send to their leaders? That thinking, though seemingly noble, is ultimately harmful to leaders and eventually to patients. No healthy, grounded leader will remain in that environment for long. The long-term consequences on culture, morale, and patient outcomes are inevitable.

The healthiest organizations understand that caring for patients and caring for the people who serve them are not competing priorities. Both matter. Leaders are part of those who serve.

Many of you have witnessed the difference a senior leader can make in the satisfaction, health, and stability of leadership teams. Two organizations may face the same challenges and the same resource limitations, yet the environments can feel completely different. Often, the difference comes down to empathy, support, and emotional intelligence. The best CEOs acknowledge challenges honestly, validate the emotional weight carried by leaders, and communicate trust. They also take practical steps, however small, to create healthier options, rhythms, and expectations. Even in constrained environments, strong leaders model what it means to care for their own souls and the souls of those they lead. They set the tone, shape what is normalized, and remind their teams that sustainable, faithful leadership is a responsibility.

Action Step 1: Establish One Non-Negotiable Rhythm of Rest

Choose one sustainable rhythm you will commit to every week, such as a protected evening with no email, a weekly Sabbath from decision-making, or a short daily moment of stillness. Communicate this boundary clearly to those around you. Faithful leadership begins with small, consistent acts of stewardship over your own soul.

Action Step 2: Name and Replace the "Martyr Model" in Your Leadership

Identify one unhealthy belief you've internalized about leadership (e.g., *"I must be available at all times"* or *"rest is selfish"*). Replace it with a healthier, faith-centered truth such as *"God does not ask me to carry what only He can sustain"* or *"rest is part of my responsibility, not a reward."* Then model this truth for your team.

Action Step 3: Build One Lifeline of Support

Choose one person or group who can walk with you such as a mentor, a peer leader, a chaplain, or a prayer partner. Commit to a simple, consistent check-in rhythm (even 15 minutes weekly). Leadership isolation accelerates burnout. Intentional support strengthens resilience.

Action Step 4: Simplify One Area of Leadership to Reduce Burden

Select one part of your leadership that consistently drains you such as decision-making, communication, staffing, documentation, or crisis response. Create a small system to streamline it: a decision pathway, a template, a checklist, or a delegated responsibility. Small efficiencies create meaningful emotional and mental relief and protect your capacity.

Reflection and Journal Prompts

1. Where do you most feel the pressure to be constantly available? Reflect on the internal beliefs, external expectations, or cultural norms that make you feel you must always be present. How do these pressures shape your leadership and your soul? What might God be inviting you to release?
2. What rhythm of rest is God inviting you to embrace in this season? Consider your current responsibilities and constraints. What form of Sabbath or stillness feels realistic yet meaningful? What barriers make it difficult and what supports might make it possible?
3. Who helps strengthen your spiritual and emotional health? Identify the mentors, peers, or colleagues who help you stay grounded. Where might you need to seek additional support? How could you intentionally cultivate a small circle of encouragement or accountability?
4. In what area of leadership do you feel the greatest mental or emotional strain? Name one part of your leadership that feels heavy or overwhelming. What small step could simplify it such as delegating, creating a template, or redefining expectations? How might letting go of perfection help lighten this load?

Lesson 8

Serve with Purpose

As Christian healthcare leaders, we are called to serve with purpose. To serve means placing others before yourself. Just as Jesus modeled humility and service, Christian leaders are called to do the same.

The term *servant leadership* is now so widely used that it risks losing some of its depth and power. At its core, however, servant leadership means leading from love, not pride, and from compassion, not control. It means viewing leadership not as a privilege to be guarded, but as a responsibility to be shared for the good of others.

Understanding Your Purpose

Purpose flows from calling and gives direction. It clarifies what you are meant to do and shows how you can best contribute to God's work in your specific context. This purpose is unique to each person. It is shaped by your field, organization, and the circumstances in which God has placed you. But one thing is certain: purpose rarely means maintaining the status quo. In healthcare especially, change is constant. New challenges arise every day. They may be clinical, operational, ethical, or emotional. The question for leaders is not just how to keep things running, but how to serve faithfully amid continual change.

DOI: 10.4324/9781003769781-9

Characteristics of Purposeful Servant Leaders

Purposeful servant leaders are often easy to recognize. They are supportive, stable, and understanding. They are authentic, peaceful, and calm. They listen well and make others feel safe, secure, and seen. These leaders focus on supporting those around them and on fostering their growth and well-being.

In times of uncertainty, they become a steady presence. They are the calm at the center of the storm. Sometimes teams simply need reassurance that everything is going to be okay, and these leaders know how to communicate that with sincerity. Much of this ability comes from emotional intelligence, the capacity to recognize and respond to the emotions of others. Purposeful servant leaders also demonstrate clarity of focus and direction for their teams. Many are viewed as transformational leaders, inspiring those around them to rise to a higher moral and professional standard.

Leading with Vision and Inspiring Others

Purposeful leaders articulate their purpose by painting a shared vision for others to follow. Change often brings fear, and the unknown can feel paralyzing. By vividly describing a better future, these leaders build a bridge in the minds of their followers, helping them imagine crossing the gap before being asked to step forward. In a later lesson, we will explore what it means to lead with vision in more detail. For now, let us reflect on two stories from Scripture that illustrate what it truly looks like to serve with purpose.

Paul: Serving with Purpose

The apostle Paul did not begin as a beloved leader. In fact, he started as a fierce opponent of the early Christian movement, actively persecuting followers of Jesus. Yet God transformed his heart and gave him a new mission, a calling to spread the gospel throughout the world. From that moment, Paul's life became a relentless pursuit of purpose, marked by courage, sacrifice, and unwavering faith.

Paul traveled thousands of miles across the Roman Empire, often facing dangers that would have terrified most people. He was shipwrecked, imprisoned, beaten, stoned, and left for dead. He endured hunger, thirst, exposure, and constant uncertainty about what would come next. And yet, through all of it, he pressed forward. Not for recognition, wealth, or comfort, but to serve God and others.

Even when alone and chained in a Roman prison, Paul wrote letters filled with hope and encouragement to the early churches he had established. These letters, now part of the New Testament, reveal a man who saw purpose in every moment of suffering. He understood that his hardships were not meaningless. They were part of a greater plan to strengthen the faith of others and advance God's kingdom.

Paul's life demonstrates that serving with purpose is not always easy or glamorous. It often involves pain, sacrifice, and opposition. Yet it also carries incredible impact. His courage continues to guide leaders today, and his faithfulness shows what it looks like to live a life fully aligned with God's calling.

Nehemiah: Serving with Purpose

Nehemiah was a cupbearer to the king of Persia, a trusted and comfortable position. Yet his heart burned with concern for his people and the city of Jerusalem. When he heard that Jerusalem's walls were broken and its gates burned, he wept. He fasted and prayed, laying his fears, sorrow, and hopes before God. Nehemiah did not react impulsively. He sought guidance, asking for courage, wisdom, and favor.

With a clear sense of purpose, Nehemiah approached King Artaxerxes. He articulated a vision of a safe and restored Jerusalem where God's people could live with dignity and hope. The king granted him resources and authority to rebuild the walls. Nehemiah's leadership began not with commanding, but with listening, discerning, and aligning his heart with God's plan.

Upon arriving in Jerusalem, Nehemiah surveyed the damage under cover of night. He saw jagged walls, broken gates, and the vulnerability of the people. Rather than despair, he gathered the people, shared a vision of restoration, assigned tasks, encouraged collaboration, and inspired hope where fear had taken root.

Opposition came swiftly. Enemies mocked, threatened, and plotted against him. Yet Nehemiah's purpose remained unshakable. He prayed, encouraged his people, and pressed forward, refusing to let fear or criticism derail God's work. Piece by piece, and wall by wall, the city was rebuilt.

By the time the walls were completed, Jerusalem was not only physically protected but spiritually renewed.

Nehemiah's story reminds us that serving with purpose requires courage, prayerful guidance, and unwavering commitment, often in the face of fear and opposition. Together, these stories remind us that purpose is not found in comfort or success, but in obedience and faithfulness. True purpose often leads us into places of challenge and growth, where we depend fully on God's strength rather than our own.

Living with Purpose Today

Just like Paul and Nehemiah, God has a purpose for your life. This purpose is rooted in your relationship with God through Jesus Christ, and He also gives each of us a vocational purpose. With a servant's heart, your task is to identify and live into that purpose. Calling may point you toward a field, but a more specific purpose often emerges through your ongoing walk with God across different seasons of life.

Living with purpose means showing up fully in the work God has entrusted to you, even when it is challenging, uncertain, or unseen by others. It means leading and serving with intention, not simply going through the motions or waiting for recognition. Purpose guides decisions, shapes priorities, and sustains you when obstacles arise.

Remember that you are not alone. God equips you with wisdom, strength, and community to walk the path He has set before you. Prayer, Scripture, and counsel from trusted mentors can illuminate your next steps. Let your actions reflect love, integrity, and humility.

Ultimately, serving with purpose is less about the tasks you accomplish and more about the transformation you bring to those you lead, the people you serve, and even yourself. Step forward with courage, trusting that God's hand guides every step. A life lived with intentionality and service becomes a testimony of His faithfulness, a light for others, and a legacy that endures far beyond any role or position.

Action Step 1: Clarify Your Purpose

Take time this week to prayerfully reflect on *why* you do what you do. Write down what initially drew you to your profession and how that connects to your faith. Ask: *How does my work serve others and honor God?* Reconnecting with this renews motivation and re-centers your daily actions around purpose rather than routine.

Action Step 2: Align Service with Purpose

Identify one way your current work or leadership can more clearly reflect your calling to serve. This could mean mentoring a struggling team member, improving the patient experience, or addressing a source of burnout in your organization. Service rooted in purpose transforms ordinary work into ministry.

Action Step 3: Lead Through Vision, Not Fear

Communicate a vision of hope to those you lead. When change brings uncertainty, speak with clarity and confidence about the direction ahead. Encourage your team by describing not just *what* you're doing, but *why* it matters. A purposeful leader helps others see God's work unfolding even in challenging seasons.

Action Step 4: Stay Grounded in Prayer and Scripture

Like Paul and Nehemiah, continually seek God's guidance. Make it a daily habit to pray for wisdom in your decisions and for the people you lead. Reflect on passages that speak to purpose and perseverance. Purpose without prayer risks pride. Prayer keeps purpose pure.

Reflection and Journal Prompts

1. In what ways am I currently serving others with humility and love, and where might pride, control, or comfort be getting in the way of true service?
2. How has my understanding of God's purpose for my work evolved over time? What season am I in right now, and what might God be asking me to focus on in this season?

3. Think of a time when you helped others see a clearer vision of what could be: at work, home, or in ministry. What did that experience teach you about leading with purpose instead of fear?
4. How can I measure my success not by outcomes or recognition, but by faithfulness to God's purpose? What daily practices can help me stay aligned with that mindset?

Lesson 9

See Your Workplace as a Mission Field

For Christian healthcare leaders, one of the most transformative shifts is learning to see your work as a form of sacred ministry. When the workplace becomes a mission field, every interaction with colleagues, patients, and teams becomes an opportunity to demonstrate compassion, integrity, and a Christlike presence. This perspective moves leadership beyond managing tasks and invites you into purposeful service. It infuses everyday work with deep spiritual meaning.

Prioritizing Mission over Margin

This mindset stands in contrast to how leadership is often approached. Many organizations emphasize financial health and sustainability above all else, at times justifying actions that conflict with Christian values. This challenge exists in both for-profit and nonprofit settings, where phrases like "no margin, no mission" are commonly used. While financial stability is essential, it becomes concerning when it begins to overshadow the spiritual and relational dimensions of leadership. Seeing your workplace as a mission field keeps the calling to serve others and reflect Christlike values at the center of your leadership. Financial health remains important, but it becomes a means to support the mission rather than the mission itself.

DOI: 10.4324/9781003769781-10

Responding with Christlike Presence

This perspective also shapes how you respond during emotionally charged encounters. Maintaining a Christlike presence in moments of anger, fear, or frustration can be challenging, but seeing your work as ministry provides grounding and clarity. Instead of reacting out of stress or self-protection, you become better able to respond with patience, compassion, and integrity. This mindset transforms difficult situations into opportunities to model Christlike care and wisdom.

Shaping Culture and Decisions

Seeing your workplace as a mission field also influences the culture you cultivate and the decisions you make. While decisions often involve financial considerations, they are rarely simple or purely transactional. A ministry mindset encourages balancing financial stewardship with compassion, ethics, and Christlike priorities. When allocating limited resources, this approach promotes creativity and discernment. It helps you make choices that honor both organizational sustainability and the well-being of those you serve.

Leadership Development and Mentorship

A mission-field mentality reshapes how you mentor and develop others. When you see your organization as a place of ministry, your approach to leadership development becomes more holistic. Staff members are not merely employees fulfilling roles, but individuals with unique stories, struggles, gifts, and callings.

Mentoring then extends beyond teaching skills or improving performance. It becomes an opportunity to shape character, nurture spiritual growth, and model Christlike leadership in everyday interactions. This perspective encourages leaders to invest intentionally in the people they serve, creating space for honest conversations, offering guidance rooted in wisdom and compassion, and affirming the God-given dignity and potential within each person. In doing so, mentorship becomes a form of ministry that supports both professional development and spiritual flourishing.

Delivering Care with Compassion

This mindset shapes the everyday delivery of care, influencing patient interactions, clinical practices, and the overall quality of service. It guides not only what leaders do but also how they train and equip frontline caregivers, emphasizing compassion, attentiveness, integrity, and respect in every encounter. When staff internalize this perspective, routine tasks become expressions of the organization's mission. Each interaction, no matter how brief, becomes an opportunity to extend dignity and kindness to patients and families. Leaders can encourage teams to offer holistic care that attends to emotional, spiritual, and physical needs, ensuring that every aspect of service reflects Christlike love.

Caring for Those Who Lead and Serve

Equally important is the well-being of staff. A mission-field mentality recognizes that the health, resilience, and support of team members directly affect their ability to serve patients and one another. Leaders who view their workplace as ministry understand that caring for their teams is not secondary. It is a primary responsibility. This includes establishing practices and policies that foster emotional support, encourage work-life balance, and offer opportunities for reflection, prayer, or spiritual renewal where appropriate. When leaders intentionally nurture staff well-being, they cultivate a healthier, more engaged team capable of delivering compassionate, Christlike care while sustaining their own purpose in ministry.

Making Decisions with Integrity Under Pressure

Healthcare leaders frequently face high-pressure situations that test their values, judgment, and composure. Adopting a mission-field mindset helps leaders navigate these moments with integrity rather than expedience. This perspective encourages thoughtful pauses, prayer, and consultation with trusted advisors before making critical decisions. By grounding choices in core principles and Christlike priorities, leaders ensure that even under stress, their actions honor both the organization's mission and the well-being of those they serve. In this way, high-stakes decision-making becomes an opportunity to model ethical, compassionate, and principled leadership.

Witness Through Leadership

As you begin to see your work as a mission field, it is important to recognize that ministry is not always explicit. While faith can be shared openly in some faith-based organizations, the most powerful witness often occurs through the way you lead and live. By modeling humility, honesty, integrity, and service, you allow Christ's love to be reflected in your actions, decisions, and interactions. Even without words, your leadership can profoundly influence the faith and values of those around you.

Leading as Ministry

Seeing your workplace as a mission field can transform every aspect of leadership, including financial stewardship, organizational decisions, patient care, staff well-being, training, mentorship, and ethical discernment. It shapes the culture you seek to build. This perspective invites you to move beyond managing tasks and calls you to lead with faith, courage, and purpose.

When leaders adopt this mindset, challenges become opportunities for ministry, routine tasks become avenues for service, and high-pressure moments become occasions to demonstrate ethical and compassionate decision-making. Your presence, actions, and choices serve as a witness to the values you hold and the faith you live out. Ultimately, seeing your workplace as a mission field reminds you that leadership is not merely about organizational success, but about the people you serve, the culture you shape, and the example you set. By intentionally integrating Christlike principles into every aspect of your work, you fulfill a higher calling: to lead in a way that honors God, uplifts others, and leaves a lasting, life-giving impact on all entrusted to your care.

Action Step 1: Begin Each Day by Intentionally Dedicating Your Work to God

Take a few moments to pray, reflect, or set a quiet intention that your leadership, decisions, and interactions will reflect Christlike compassion and integrity throughout the day.

Action Step 2: Identify One Relationship or Area of Influence to Intentionally Invest in this Week

Choose a colleague, staff member, or team where you can model ministry-minded leadership through listening, encouragement, mentorship, or support.

Action Step 3: Review an Upcoming Decision Through a Mission-First Lens

Ask yourself: *How does this choice reflect Christlike values? Who is affected? What does wise stewardship look like?* Use these questions to guide at least one real decision you make in the coming week.

Action Step 4: Create Small Rhythms That Support Spiritual Presence in Your Leadership

Incorporate practices such as brief pauses before difficult conversations, end-of-day reflection, gratitude journaling, or walking rounds with intentional attentiveness. These micro-rhythms help anchor your leadership in a ministry mindset.

Reflection and Journal Prompts

1. Where do I most clearly see my workplace as a mission field right now, and where do I struggle to view it that way? Reflect on what helps you

embrace a ministry mindset and what obstacles such as stress, culture, fear, or habits, make it difficult.

2. How have my recent decisions reflected or failed to reflect Christlike values? Consider a few key decisions from the past month. What guided them? What might I approach differently with a mission-first perspective?
3. Who in my workplace might God be inviting me to see, support, or encourage more intentionally? Think about individuals such as staff, colleagues, or patients whose stories, burdens, or gifts may need your attention or compassionate presence.
4. In what ways is God shaping my character through the pressures and responsibilities of my role? Reflect on how challenges, conflicts, or difficult moments are forming you spiritually. What is God teaching you about leadership, humility, resilience, or trust?

Lesson 10

Build Micro-Cultures of Hope

As Christians, we are called to turn away from cultural values that lead to emptiness rather than true fulfillment. This applies to both our personal and professional lives. In healthcare, the prevailing culture is often marked by relentless pace, burnout, and an emphasis on outcomes over relationships. Yet we are called to build something different: micro-cultures of hope, compassion, emotional well-being, and respect for human dignity that reflect the love of Christ in practical, transformative ways.

What Is a Micro-Culture?

A micro-culture is a small, intentionally cultivated environment within a larger system, such as a hospital, clinic, or health network. It embodies values that may differ from or even quietly challenge the broader culture. While we may not have the power to transform the entire healthcare system, we can shape the spaces we lead. Each micro-culture becomes a testimony to what is possible when Christian values are lived out, even within systems that feel broken. For example, the dominant culture in healthcare often shows itself through rushed appointments, caregiver burnout, transactional interactions, and an emphasis on metrics over people. In contrast, a culture of hope creates space to truly listen, honor each person's dignity, and care for staff well-being.

In many systems, patients are reduced to statistics, and staff can feel expendable. Yet we have both the opportunity and the responsibility to humanize care by prioritizing empathy, slowing down to connect, and

DOI: 10.4324/9781003769781-11

valuing presence over performance. Sometimes this means pausing to truly see a patient, offering a word of encouragement to a weary colleague, or creating a moment of prayer in the midst of a demanding day. These small, repeated choices begin to transform the atmosphere around us. When we lead with this mindset, our work begins to mirror the ministry of Jesus.

Following the Example of Jesus

Jesus Himself lived and led in a countercultural way, creating micro-cultures of hope and healing wherever He went. He challenged both religious and societal norms, healing on the Sabbath, touching lepers, and speaking with the Samaritan woman. He consistently prioritized relationships over rules and compassion over condemnation. Jesus did not passively accept the culture He was born into. He transformed it from within. Through His actions, He modeled what it means to build a culture rooted in love, inclusion, and care for the broken and marginalized.

The following verse reminds us that we are not meant to simply adopt the values of the surrounding culture. Transformation begins in our minds. This includes our perspectives, priorities, and the way we approach every decision.

> Do not conform to the pattern of this world, but be transformed by the renewing of your mind.
>
> Romans 12:2 (NIV)

Leadership as Cultural Stewardship

Christian leadership is more than managing people. It is an act of cultural stewardship. Leaders are responsible not only for results but also for the spiritual and emotional environment they cultivate. When we adopt this perspective, we begin to see that our influence extends beyond daily operations. We are creating spaces where others can encounter God through love, kindness, and genuine presence. Leadership, then, becomes a sacred calling. It is an invitation to resist the dehumanizing tendencies of modern systems and usher in a divine alternative. To lead as a Christian is to cultivate environments that reflect the heart of God, not the values of a broken world.

The Role of the Holy Spirit

As you reframe your calling, remember the vital role of the Holy Spirit in shaping a micro-culture of hope. The Spirit produces the very environment we long to see, marked by love, joy, peace, patience, kindness, goodness, faithfulness, gentleness, and self-control (Galatians 5:22–23). When we invite the Spirit into our leadership and workplaces, we receive divine guidance and strength in this sacred work. The Spirit softens hearts, reshapes perspectives, and guides conversations in ways we never could on our own.

Amid the size and complexity of today's systems, it is easy to feel powerless. But God is greater than the brokenness around us and is always working for our good. True transformation begins in the heart of each leader who says yes to God's Spirit at work within and around them. In this way, we begin to reshape entire cultures of care.

A Prayer for Culture Makers

> Lord, help us to build a culture of hope and healing in our workplaces.
> Let every conversation, every decision, and every interaction reflect Your love and grace.
> May we be culture makers, just as Jesus was in His life and ministry.
> Amen.

Action Step 1: Intentionally Create a Micro-Culture Reflecting Christian Values

Identify the core values you want to embody, such as hope, compassion, dignity, and emotional well-being, and deliberately cultivate these within your team or workplace. Design daily practices and norms (e.g., slowing down to listen, encouraging prayer, celebrating small wins) that reinforce this culture despite external pressures.

Action Step 2: Model Emotional Openness and Authentic Connection

Foster genuine relationships through vulnerability and empathy. Encourage open conversations about struggles and hopes, creating safe spaces where both staff and patients feel seen and valued beyond their roles or diagnoses.

Action Step 3: Lead as a Cultural Steward Guided by the Holy Spirit

Embrace your leadership role as a spiritual calling to nurture an environment where God's love and grace are evident. Regularly seek the Holy Spirit's guidance to cultivate fruits like kindness, patience, and self-control in decisions and interactions, recognizing that you cannot do this work alone.

Action Step 4: Reject Dehumanizing Norms and Advocate for Person-Centered Care

Actively resist and challenge cultural pressures that reduce people to metrics. Prioritize presence over performance by advocating for policies and practices that honor each person's dignity and promote well-being.

Reflection and Journal Prompts

1. What values currently shape your daily work and leadership? Are these aligned with a culture of hope, compassion, and dignity? Where might you need to shift your focus?
2. In what ways do you see the larger culture dehumanizing people? How have you, consciously or unconsciously, bought into this culture? What steps can you take to resist it and create a micro-culture in your sphere?
3. How do you currently invite the Holy Spirit into your leadership and work environment? What practical habits or prayers could help you more intentionally steward the spiritual culture of your workplace?
4. Reflect on your recent interactions at work. How often do you prioritize authentic connection and emotional openness? What barriers prevent deeper relationships, and how might you overcome them to build a more hopeful, compassionate micro-culture?

STRENGTHENING THE HEART AND SPIRIT

II

Lesson 11

Cultivate Inner Resilience

Just as athletes train their bodies for the race ahead, Christian healthcare leaders must prepare their hearts and minds for the journey set before them. This preparation begins with cultivating inner resilience, which is vital in high-stress healthcare environments. Practices like meditation, mindfulness, and breathwork help calm the mind, ground the body, and foster spiritual clarity. In that stillness, we become more aware of God's presence and better able to discern His guidance. As Scripture reminds us:

> Be still before the Lord and wait patiently for him.
>
> Psalm 37:7 (NIV)

These disciplines help us live out this verse, nurturing spiritual stillness while improving mental and physical well-being. Though embraced across various traditions, their purpose is universal: calming the nervous system, reducing stress, and cultivating awareness. When practiced intentionally, they empower us to remain anchored in peace throughout the day. For Christian leaders, these practices can also be integrated with faith, turning moments of stillness into opportunities for prayer, reflection, and renewed spiritual strength.

Faith-Integrated Practices

- **Prayer before meditation**. Before beginning a traditional meditation, take a moment to pray, asking God to make His presence known during this time of stillness.

DOI: 10.4324/9781003769781-13

- **Mindful pauses.** Instead of reacting in the moment, pause and take slow, deep breaths while focusing on a phrase such as, "Be still and know that I am God" (Psalm 46:10, NIV).
- **Evening prayer walks.** A daily evening walk can reduce stress and center the mind. Using this time for prayer can transform the walk into a regular time with God.
- **Lectio Divina.** Sometimes called "Christian meditation," Lectio Divina (Latin for "Divine Reading") is a spiritual practice that differs from traditional meditation. Unlike traditional meditation, which often focuses on emptying the mind, Lectio Divina fills the heart with God's Word and invites you to listen for His personal voice. It engages Scripture not merely for knowledge but for communion and transformation.

Lectio Divina Steps

- **Lectio (Read).** Slowly read a short Bible passage, noting any word or phrase that stands out.
- **Meditatio (Reflect).** Reflect on what God might be saying to you.
- **Oratio (Respond).** Speak with God in prayer, honestly and openly.
- **Contemplatio (Rest).** Sit quietly in God's presence, simply being with Him.

Whether practiced traditionally or through a Christian lens, these disciplines regulate emotions, quiet the mind, and create space for peace. They help leaders act from grace, rather than reacting from fear or frustration. One of the most powerful practices may be developing a daily habit of morning and evening meditation. I recommend 20 minutes before breakfast and dinner, though you can adjust the timing as needed. Adding a short meditation during a lunch break can enhance the effect. These habits build not only resilience but also a calm presence, the kind of peace that defines great leaders.

Becoming the Calm in the Storm

Calm, centered leaders are better equipped to handle stress and the emotionally charged situations common in healthcare. These leaders remain steady under pressure, like the calm at the center of the storm. It's easy to assume that this kind of composure is a natural trait, but it is often the result of intentional discipline and consistent mental conditioning. Strong leaders develop habits that keep them grounded, responsive, and clear-minded in challenging moments. These practices include:

- **Self-awareness.** Recognizing emotional triggers and thought patterns as they arise.
- **Pausing before acting.** Creating space to choose your response rather than reacting impulsively.
- **Pattern-breaking.** Interrupting automatic reactions and replacing them with grounded, intentional responses.
- **Mental reframing.** Shifting your perspective to see challenges not as threats, but as opportunities for growth.

At the heart of all this is a simple but powerful principle: decide in advance how you will respond rather than reacting impulsively in the moment. Over time, these practices cultivate the emotional strength and spiritual depth that define Christ-centered leadership, even in the most demanding circumstances. In doing so, you not only steady yourself but become a living example of Christ's peace in the midst of chaos.

Action Step 1: Commit to a Daily 20-Minute Meditation or Guided Relaxation Practice

Set aside 20 minutes each morning for a breath-focused meditation or a guided relaxation. Use a timer or app and allow your body and mind to settle. These moments of stillness calm your nervous system, reduce stress, and create space to notice God's presence.

Action Step 2: Pause and Pray Before Difficult Conversations or Decisions

When stress rises, create a *sacred pause*. Whether it's a moment, an hour, or even a day, step away if you can. Breathe deeply, and ask God for clarity, wisdom, and grace. This intentional pause can reset your tone, mindset, and presence, which prepares you to respond, not just react.

Action Step 3: Practice a Daily Mental Reframe

Throughout your day, when you encounter a challenge or frustration, pause and reframe it as a potential growth opportunity. Ask yourself: *How might God be using this to shape me or someone else?* Jot down your insight when you can, and return to it later for deeper reflection. This ongoing practice can shift your perspective and build spiritual resilience.

Action Step 4: Establish a Weekly Lectio Divina Practice

Choose one evening per week to practice Lectio Divina with a short passage of Scripture (e.g., a psalm or a gospel story). Let God speak into your heart without rushing. Reflect, pray, and listen.

Reflection and Journal Prompts

1. When I feel overwhelmed, what is my usual internal response? What does that reveal about my current state of resilience?
2. Which spiritual practice helps me feel most connected to God right now? Is there a practice you feel drawn to deepen or return to?
3. Am I leading from peace or pressure? What would it look like to lead more consistently from a place of calm, trust, and clarity?
4. What kind of presence do I bring into the room? What might need to shift internally to align that presence with Christ's peace and compassion?

Lesson 12

Establish Rhythms of Peace

Lasting peace in life and leadership doesn't happen by accident. It grows from intentional rhythms that shape your mind, heart, and body. Just as inner resilience is strengthened through deliberate practices, rhythms of peace carry calm and clarity into every part of your day.

For Christian healthcare leaders, these rhythms are both practical and spiritual. They create space to release stress, reconnect with God, and renew your energy so you can lead with steadiness, compassion, and wisdom. In this lesson, we will explore simple, actionable practices that cultivate inner peace. These include letting go rituals, mindful pauses, prayerful movement, and digital boundaries. By establishing these rhythms, you not only strengthen your own well-being but also shape a culture of balance and hope for those you lead.

Letting Go at the End of the Day

Consider a simple letting go ritual to transition from work into rest. For example, before bed or when arriving home, write down lingering thoughts, worries, or unresolved issues. This practice signals to your brain: *I've acknowledged this, and it's in God's hands for now.* This act of release promotes emotional resilience and allows you to truly rest, body, mind, and spirit.

DOI: 10.4324/9781003769781-14

Leaving Work Behind

Build a brief transition moment as you leave work behind. For example:

- Sit in your car and take a few slow, deep breaths
- Pray, "Lord, I leave the weight of today in Your hands"
- Listen to worship music during your commute to reset your focus

These small pauses act as spiritual and emotional reset buttons, helping you reconnect with God before stepping into your home or next responsibility.

Practicing Gratitude

Gratitude shifts your mindset from stress to appreciation. Each evening, write down a few things you are thankful for, such as:

- Family and friends
- Your home
- Kindness you experienced
- Small wins
- Glimpses of God's grace

Over time, this cultivates peace and perspective, helping you focus on God's faithfulness rather than daily stress.

Centering in Scripture

Choose a short verse, such as:

> Be still, and know that I am God.
>
> Psalm 46:10 (NIV)

Repeat it slowly as you breathe deeply. Let each word settle into your heart. Allow the truth of Scripture to still your mind, ground your spirit, and draw you into God's presence. This simple practice becomes a sacred pause where peace takes root, and your soul remembers who is truly in control.

The Mental Drop Zone

In addition to spiritual practices, there are practical tools you can use throughout the day to stay clear-minded. Keep a running list, either in a journal or a digital notes app, where you write down:

- Tasks
- Concerns
- Ideas

This clears your mental space so you can stay focused without feeling overwhelmed. Unlike your end-of-day ritual, this tool helps maintain clarity during the day.

Establishing Digital Boundaries

Set a firm time each day to stop checking emails or work messages. Pair this boundary with a simple prayer:

> God, help me release what is unfinished. I trust You with what remains.

This reinforces the truth that your value is not tied to productivity and encourages emotional separation between work and rest.

Evening Prayer Walks

Take a short evening walk to release physical tension. Use it as a form of moving prayer. Let each step be a way of exhaling stress and inhaling peace. This simple rhythm strengthens your body, clears your mind, and cultivates spiritual awareness.

Leading a Culture of Balance and Compassion

Once these rhythms begin bearing fruit in your life, consider sharing them with your team. Emotional and spiritual well-being is not just personal. It is cultural. In many healthcare environments, urgency and constant output are normalized. Staff often skip meals, breaks, or even restroom visits to meet patient needs. Yet this model is not sustainable. A culture built on overextension leads to burnout, frustration, and diminished care. Encourage small pauses during the day, such as:

- Moments of stillness over lunch
- Short breathwork exercises
- A quiet space with Scripture or prayer

These small shifts can transform individuals and positively influence the overall spirit of your workplace.

Honoring Seasons of Life

Work–life balance looks different depending on a person's season of life. An empty nester may choose longer hours for connection and purpose. Someone with young children may need more time at home. Effective leaders recognize and honor these differences, offering flexibility and empathy where possible.

Modeling Rhythms from the Top

Leadership sets the tone. If a leader models workaholism, that mindset trickles down. But if you model balance, boundaries, and rhythms of peace, others will follow your lead. As a Christian healthcare leader, you are uniquely positioned to shape a culture that honors both human limits and God's strength.

Running with Endurance

The race you're running is not just physical or mental. It is deeply spiritual. Strengthening your mind and spirit requires intention, patience, and grace. You are called to lead others, but also to lead yourself with wisdom and compassion. Despite the demands of healthcare, stillness is a necessity. By cultivating peace and resilience, you create a sanctuary where healing can flourish not just for patients but for your entire team.

An Invitation to Peace

Let this chapter be an invitation to slow down and to listen more deeply to God, to yourself, and to those you lead.

Choose one rhythm of peace to begin practicing this week. Whether it is a letting go ritual, digital boundaries, or a short evening walk, begin somewhere. Start small and stay faithful. When you nurture your own soul, you build the foundation for authentic leadership rooted in peace and purpose. Run this race with endurance, knowing you do not run alone, but with the steady presence of God guiding every step.

Action Step 1: Take a Prayerful Evening Walk

Choose 2–3 evenings this week to take a short walk after work. Use it as a time to release the day's tension, breathe deeply, and connect with God. Let each step be a way of exhaling stress and inhaling peace.

Action Step 2: Establish a Digital Boundary

Set a clear time in the evening when you will stop checking work emails or messages. Pair it with a brief prayer or moment of release, reminding yourself that your worth is not tied to productivity.

Action Step 3: Begin a Mental Drop Zone

Start a running list (either in a journal or a digital notes app) where you write down lingering thoughts, tasks, or worries throughout the day. Use this tool to clear mental clutter and stay grounded.

Action Step 4: Introduce a Gratitude Practice

Each evening, write down 3 things you're grateful for. Include moments of kindness, small victories, or ways you saw God's grace during the day. Do this consistently for the next 7 days.

Reflection and Journal Prompts

1. What weight am I still carrying from today that God is inviting me to release? Write honestly about any stress, pressure, or unresolved issues. End your entry with a written prayer of release.
2. How does my current rhythm between work and rest impact my peace? Reflect on your current habits and whether they restore you or leave you feeling depleted. What changes could help bring better balance?
3. Which rhythm of peace resonates most with me right now, and why? Consider which practice (letting go ritual, Scripture centering, prayer walk, etc.) feels most needed in your life today.
4. How might my personal rhythms influence the culture of those I lead? Reflect on your leadership. In what ways are you modeling peace and balance? Where might you be unintentionally modeling burnout?

Lesson 13

Prioritize Rhythms of Rest and Renewal

Rhythms of rest and renewal are among the most essential practices for healthcare leaders, supporting both effective leadership and long-term sustainability. Yet many leaders neglect this form of self-care. Even so, rest is not a luxury but a spiritual necessity rooted in Scripture. God Himself established the rhythm of Sabbath, modeling rest on the seventh day of creation and later embedding it within the Ten Commandments. Rest is not optional. It is woven into God's design for human flourishing.

How Leaders Shape Culture

What leaders model at the top inevitably becomes part of the organizational culture. Their behaviors shape expectations, norms, and daily patterns that ripple through every level of the organization. Unfortunately, many leaders today have advanced not because they demonstrated balanced, healthy leadership, but because they could endure more than others. In a broken healthcare system, endurance is often rewarded above empathy, compassion, or relational skill. Leaders shaped by this system may develop workaholic tendencies, hold unrealistic expectations, and adopt a resigned belief that "this is just the way it is." Over time, this belief hardens into a prevailing mindset:

DOI: 10.4324/9781003769781-15

- "There isn't enough money to staff adequately."
- "Workloads are unmanageable."
- "Burnout is inevitable, and staff must be continually replaced."

A Different Way of Leading

Most healthcare professionals have witnessed this kind of leadership firsthand. These individuals may not always display the interpersonal skills, compassion, or presence you would hope for. Yet in many cases, they are doing the best they can within the limitations of the system. This is precisely why Christian healthcare leaders have the opportunity and responsibility to lead differently by modeling sustainable, compassionate leadership.

Steps Toward Healthy Rhythms

While there is no quick fix to the systemic challenges of healthcare, leaders can take small, intentional steps to stay spiritually healthy and care for those they lead. Earlier lessons explored cultivating inner resilience and rhythms of peace. Rhythms of rest and renewal are equally essential. When leaders prioritize these rhythms, they begin to notice countless small opportunities in daily decisions to extend grace, encourage rest, and create healthier patterns for themselves and others.

Jesus' Invitation to Rest

Scripture consistently emphasizes the importance of rest and renewal as part of God's design for human life. God's establishment of the Sabbath serves as both permission and promise, as if to say, "You may rest, and you will be sustained." Jesus reinforces this with an open invitation:

> Come to me, all you who are weary and burdened, and I will give you rest. Take my yoke upon you and learn from me, for I am gentle and humble in heart, and you will find rest for your souls. For my yoke is easy and my burden is light.
>
> Matthew 11:28–30 (NIV)

If God the Father and Jesus both elevate rest as essential to spiritual and emotional well-being, how can we justify ignoring it? As Christian leaders, we must model rest in our own lives and extend it graciously to others. This will often run counter to prevailing healthcare culture, but it is profoundly impactful. Leading with a rest-first mindset does not mean abandoning stewardship or patient care. Rather, it recognizes that every organization, including acute care settings, contains micro-opportunities to offer rest, lighten burdens, and humanize the work in small but meaningful ways.

Practical Ways Leaders Can Model and Extend Rest

Practical examples include:

- Allowing brief pauses during intense shifts (e.g., encouraging a team member to take a five-minute moment to breathe, reset, or pray).
- Setting healthy communication boundaries, such as device-free meetings or clearly stating that team members are not expected to read or respond to emails after hours.
- Actively redistributing workload when a staff member is overwhelmed, rather than allowing silent suffering to persist.
- Publicly affirming the importance of rest in team huddles, leadership rounds, or organizational communications.
- Normalizing the use of PTO and Sabbath-like rest by taking it yourself and encouraging others to do the same.
- Building small rhythms of renewal into department routines (brief gratitude check-ins, moments of silence, team blessings, shared reflection).
- Extending grace when someone is exhausted, recognizing that compassion fatigue often signals a deeper need for rest rather than a lack of commitment.

Embedding Rest into Organizational Identity

Rest can be embedded not only in personal habits but also in an organization's mission, values, and daily operations. When a commitment to well-being is articulated and actively supported by senior leadership, it becomes part of the organization's long-term identity. A central theme of this book is the conviction that the health and well-being of both leaders and frontline staff must be prioritized alongside the care of those they serve. Keep this principle in mind as you assess the culture, processes, and systems within your organization.

A Spirit-Led Approach to Renewal

There are many meaningful ways to prioritize rhythms of rest and renewal. One of the most effective is simply having honest conversations with leadership teams and frontline staff. They often know best what would help them experience rest, recovery, and sustainability in their roles. When leaders invite their ideas, two things happen: creative and practical solutions emerge, and the pressure lifts from the leader to generate every idea alone.

It is also essential to recognize that we need God's wisdom to make these changes within the realities and constraints of healthcare organizations. This includes acknowledging the role of the Holy Spirit in rest, renewal, and transformation. By asking God to guide you and inviting the Spirit to shape your team, culture, and organization, you affirm your dependence on His strength rather than your own.

Finally, it is reassuring to remember that anything we consistently prioritize can change over time. Even small, faithful steps toward healthier rhythms make a difference. Prioritizing rest and renewal is not only one of the most important practices for your spiritual well-being; it is also one of the greatest gifts you can offer to those you lead.

Action Step 1: Establish One Weekly Period of Rest

Choose a specific time each week, such as a few hours, half a day, or a full day, completely set aside for rest, prayer, reflection, or spiritual renewal. Protect this time as you would any important appointment and avoid work or other obligations during it.

Action Step 2: Model Healthy Boundaries for Your Team

Select a boundary you can practice consistently, such as not checking or responding to emails after work hours, holding device-free meetings, or taking your full PTO. Communicate your approach clearly so your team sees it modeled in daily practice.

Action Step 3: Invite Your Team into a Conversation About Renewal

Hold a brief discussion asking your team what small practices would help them experience more rest and sustainability in their daily work. Capture their ideas and implement at least one practical suggestion immediately.

Action Step 4: Implement One Small Routine to Encourage Rest

Identify a repeatable practice in your department that encourages recovery and renewal, such as a brief pause before rounds or offering coverage for short breaks. Embed this practice into the normal workflow so it becomes part of the culture.

Reflection and Journal Prompts

1. Reflect on your current rhythms of rest and renewal. Which practices help you recharge spiritually, emotionally, and physically? Which areas need improvement? Write down one change you could make this week to prioritize rest.
2. Think about the way you currently model rest for your team. How do your behaviors, communication patterns, and visible habits influence the culture around rest? What is one boundary you could set this week to model healthier rhythms?
3. Consider your team or department. What are small, practical opportunities to support rest, renewal, or spiritual encouragement for others? Brainstorm three ideas you could implement in the next month.

4. Reflect on how you rely on God and invite the Holy Spirit into your leadership. How can you more intentionally seek guidance, strength, and wisdom to cultivate rhythms of rest for yourself and your team? Write a short prayer or action plan for this week.

Lesson 14

Practice Humility

One hallmark of Christian leadership is humility. It means putting others before yourself, serving faithfully, and recognizing that influence is a responsibility, not a privilege. Humility is a mindset that acknowledges your limitations, values others, and places the greater good above personal recognition. Key aspects of humility include:

- **Self-Awareness.** Understanding your strengths and weaknesses honestly.
- **Respect for Others.** Valuing people's perspectives, contributions, and dignity.
- **Teachability.** Being willing to learn, admit mistakes, and accept guidance.
- **Service Orientation.** Putting others' needs ahead of your own.
- **Gratitude and Perspective.** Recognizing that accomplishments often involve help from others.

In Christian leadership, humility is the foundation for servant leadership, reflecting the example of Jesus, who led by serving rather than seeking status or power. Humility shapes how we lead teams, make decisions, and model Christlike character in every interaction.

DOI: 10.4324/9781003769781-16

Humility in Practice

Humility can look like:

- **Admitting Mistakes.** Owning errors and learning from them.
- **Seeking Feedback.** Inviting input, even when it feels uncomfortable.
- **Prioritizing Others' Needs.** Putting team members, patients, or colleagues before personal gain.
- **Listening More Than Speaking.** Valuing others' perspectives before asserting your own.
- **Recognizing Others' Contributions.** Giving credit to those who help achieve success.

These practices are more than professional skills. They reflect a Christ-centered approach to leadership. For Christian leaders, humility means admitting you don't have all the answers, valuing others' input, serving faithfully without seeking recognition, and trusting God rather than relying solely on yourself. It calls leaders to put others first, cultivate community, and reflect the character of Christ in every action.

Humility in Scripture

These principles are not just theoretical. They are exemplified in Scripture by leaders who modeled servant-hearted leadership.

Moses

Moses was chosen by God to lead the Israelites out of slavery and into the Promised Land. Despite this enormous responsibility, he is described as:

> … a very humble man, more humble than anyone else on the face of the earth.
>
> Numbers 12:3 (NIV)

From the beginning, Moses admitted he did not have all the answers:

> Who am I that I should go to Pharaoh and bring the Israelites out of Egypt?
>
> Exodus 3:11 (NIV)

He also expressed fear of speaking:

> Moses said to the Lord, 'Pardon your servant, Lord. I have never been eloquent, neither in the past nor since you have spoken to your servant. I am slow of speech and tongue.
>
> Exodus 4:10 (NIV)

Throughout his leadership, Moses consistently sought God's direction, delegated responsibility to capable leaders, and prioritized the well-being of the people over personal recognition.

Jesus

Jesus provides the ultimate example of humility. As the Son of God, He could have demanded honor, yet He chose to serve others selflessly. Just before His crucifixion, He performed a task normally reserved for servants:

> Now that I, your Lord and Teacher, have washed your feet, you also should wash one another's feet. I have set you an example that you should do as I have done for you.
>
> John 13:14–15 (NIV)

Through this act, Jesus showed that leadership is not about status or authority but about serving others, prioritizing their needs, and modeling a servant's heart. Today, leaders can follow His example by trusting God, relying on those He places around them, and leading with hearts focused on service rather than personal gain.

Why Humility Matters

Humility is essential for three reasons:

1. It reminds you that you don't have all the answers and that you need others to partner with you.
2. It frees you from shouldering burdens alone, allowing God's guidance and Spirit to work through you.

3. It reflects the example of Jesus Christ, who modeled service and selfless leadership.

Evaluate your actions through this lens. It is easy to be influenced by pride, ego, or power. This is especially true when under pressure or in moments of fear, anger, or insecurity. In these times, pause, re-center, and reflect on this passage:

> Do not love the world or anything in the world. If anyone loves the world, love for the Father is not in them. For everything in the world—the lust of the flesh, the lust of the eyes, and the pride of life—comes not from the Father but from the world. The world and its desires pass away, but whoever does the will of God lives forever.
>
> 1 John 2:15–17 (NIV)

A Daily Commitment to Humility

Serving with humility is a daily practice. True Christian leadership is measured not by accolades but by faithfulness, compassion, and the courage to put others first. By following the examples of Moses and Jesus and resisting worldly pride, we embrace leadership that honors God, uplifts others, and makes a lasting impact.

Closing Prayer

Lord, teach me to walk in humility each day.
When pride or self-interest rises in my heart,
remind me to serve others first and rely on Your guidance.
Keep my words gentle, my actions selfless, and my heart teachable.
May my life and leadership reflect Your love,
and may others see Your grace shining through me.
Amen.

Action Step 1: Seek Feedback Regularly

Invite honest input from colleagues, team members, and mentors. Listen carefully, reflect on their insights, and adjust your approach without defensiveness.

Action Step 2: Acknowledge Others' Contributions

Give credit where it's due. Celebrate the successes of your team and recognize the efforts of those who support your work.

Action Step 3: Serve in Practical Ways

Look for opportunities to take on tasks that benefit others, even if they are small or "behind the scenes." Demonstrating service in action reinforces humility.

Action Step 4: Practice Self-Reflection Daily

Set aside time each day to reflect on your motives, decisions, and interactions. Ask God to reveal areas where pride or self-interest may be influencing your leadership.

Reflection and Journal Prompts

1. When I reflect on my leadership this week, where did pride or self-interest influence my decisions, and how could I have responded more humbly?
2. Who in my team or community deserves recognition that I may have overlooked, and how can I intentionally honor their contributions?
3. In what specific ways did I put others' needs before my own recently, and where could I serve more faithfully or selflessly?
4. How have I relied on God's guidance in my leadership this week, and where might I be leaning too heavily on my own understanding?

Lesson 15

Lead with Integrity

Leading in healthcare as a Christian begins with integrity. It is both a personal quality and a way of living marked by honesty and ethical wholeness. At its core, it means doing the right thing, even when no one is watching. Integrity expresses itself in several ways:

- **Honesty.** Speaking truthfully and transparently in all circumstances.
- **Consistency.** Aligning your actions with your values and principles across all situations.
- **Moral Courage.** Making difficult choices that uphold ethical standards, even under pressure.
- **Wholeness.** Being the same person privately and publicly with a unified and authentic character.

For Christian leaders, integrity means reflecting God's truth and justice in decision-making, treating others with fairness and respect, and allowing faith to guide both professional and personal life. In practice, integrity can look like:

- Advocating for patients or staff, even when it conflicts with financial or administrative pressures.
- Being transparent with staff, patients, and families.
- Admitting mistakes and taking responsibility rather than deflecting blame.

DOI: 10.4324/9781003769781-17

In short, integrity is the alignment of values, beliefs, and actions. It is the bridge between conviction (what you believe) and trustworthy leadership (how you act), guiding every decision you make as a Christian leader.

Integrity in Scripture: The Example of Joseph

Joseph's life in Egypt is a powerful example of integrity under pressure. He was the favorite son of Jacob, which caused jealousy among his brothers. They sold him into slavery, and he was taken to Egypt, far from his family and everything familiar. Despite these hardships, Joseph remained faithful to God and consistently acted with honesty and moral courage. He became a trusted servant in the household of Potiphar, an Egyptian official. When Potiphar's wife tried to seduce him, Joseph refused, saying:

> No one is greater in this house than I am. My master has withheld nothing from me except you, because you are his wife. How then could I do such a wicked thing and sin against God?
>
> Genesis 39:9 (NIV)

By refusing her advances, Joseph faced great personal risk. He was falsely accused and imprisoned, yet his integrity never wavered. Even in prison, he remained truthful, trusted God, and faithfully carried out the responsibilities entrusted to him.

Eventually, Joseph rose to become second-in-command over all Egypt, overseeing the nation's resources during a severe famine. He managed Pharaoh's food supply wisely, treated people fairly, and saved countless lives. Throughout, his actions aligned with God's purposes, demonstrating consistency, moral courage, and wholeness.

Here is the lesson for Christian healthcare leaders:

- Integrity is often revealed in quiet moments when no one is watching.
- It builds trust and credibility over time, enabling leaders to serve effectively and honor God.
- Like Joseph, leaders may face pressure, temptation, or misunderstanding, but integrity ensures that every decision reflects Christlike character.

Consider this passage as well:

> Whoever can be trusted with very little can also be trusted with much, and whoever is dishonest with very little will also be dishonest with much.
>
> Luke 16:10 (NIV)

This verse reminds us that integrity is not just about dramatic decisions, but about the small choices that shape our character over time. In healthcare leadership, it shows up in daily actions: how we treat staff, interact with patients, manage resources, and follow policies. Consistently acting with honesty and faithfulness, even in minor matters, prepares us to be trusted with greater responsibilities.

As you lead with integrity, ground your decisions in Christlike virtues such as love, patience, humility, and kindness. Let these qualities shape not only what you do, but how you do it. As a result, your leadership will quietly reflect the heart of Christ to those around you.

Closing Prayer

> Lord, help me to lead with integrity that reflects Your heart.
> When life feels uncertain and the world grows impatient,
> teach me to respond with kindness, patience, and humility.
> Keep my motives pure, my actions consistent, and my words gracious.
> May my leadership be steady and compassionate,
> so that others see not my strength, but Yours working through me.
> Amen.

Action Step 1: Model Transparency in Daily Decisions

Make a conscious effort this week to communicate openly with your team, especially about difficult decisions. Explain not only *what* you decided, but *why*, to build a culture of trust and shared values.

Action Step 2: Align Policies with Principles

Review one policy or practice in your organization or department and ask: *Does this reflect fairness, compassion, and integrity?* If not, begin a conversation about how it can be improved.

Action Step 3: Admit and Own Mistakes Quickly

When you fall short, even in small matters, choose honesty over defensiveness. Acknowledge the mistake, make it right, and use it as a teaching moment for your team.

Action Step 4: Practice "Integrity Habits" Daily

End each day by asking yourself: *Did my actions today reflect Christ's character?* Choose one area (truthfulness, fairness, humility, or consistency) to focus on each week and build accountability with a trusted colleague or mentor.

Reflection and Journal Prompts

1. In what areas of my leadership am I most tempted to compromise, perhaps for convenience, approval, or results? How can I strengthen my resolve to do what is right, even when it's costly?
2. How does my relationship with Christ shape my daily leadership decisions? Where do I rely on my own strength rather than His guidance?
3. How might my integrity, or lack of it, influence those I lead? What do I want others to see about Christ through the way I lead?
4. Recall a time when your integrity was tested. What did you learn about yourself, your faith, and God's faithfulness through that experience?

Lesson 16

Be Strong and Courageous

Strength in Christian leadership is often misunderstood. It is not dominance, control, or emotional hardness. Real strength involves serving others, making difficult decisions, and choosing what is right even when it comes at personal cost. Courage shows up not only in bold action, but in the willingness to do what is emotionally challenging, ethically demanding, or quietly faithful.

Healthcare leadership requires this kind of courage every day. In a system marked by constant pressure, burnout, and uncertainty, simply stepping into a leadership role takes strength. It is no surprise that leadership turnover is high. In some organizations, CEOs remain in their roles for only one or two years. These positions have become increasingly unsustainable, yet remain deeply necessary.

So, pause here for a moment. If you are leading in healthcare, you are already demonstrating courage. By choosing to serve, you have stepped into a demanding space with the hope of making a difference. You are working within a broken system, not because it is easy, but because people matter. Caregivers matter. Patients matter. And that choice reflects both strength and calling.

You do not have to be perfect. You will not be able to fix every systemic problem you encounter. That has never been the measure of success for Christian leadership. It is also normal to feel afraid. Scripture does not deny fear. It speaks directly into it. But remember what God told Joshua:

DOI: 10.4324/9781003769781-18

> Have I not commanded you? Be strong and courageous. Do not be afraid; do not be discouraged, for the Lord your God will be with you wherever you go.
>
> Joshua 1:9 (NIV)

If God has called you, He is with you. You can rely on His strength, His support, and His power to carry out His plan.

> Being confident of this, that he who began a good work in you will carry it on to completion until the day of Christ Jesus.
>
> Philippians 1:6 (NIV)

God began this work in you. He moved your heart to serve and lead in healthcare. He will not abandon you. That does not mean you must remain in your current role forever. Every role has its season. In this season, you have the opportunity to lead and to make a lasting difference. God will guide your path, and while you are in this position, He will empower you.

> For the Spirit God gave us does not make us timid, but gives us power, love and self-discipline.
>
> 2 Timothy 1:7 (NIV)

The Realities of Healthcare Leadership

Healthcare leadership is demanding and often overwhelming. You are responsible for patient safety while navigating staffing shortages, burnout, complex regulations, legal risks, tight budgets, and constant organizational change. Long hours, ethical dilemmas, and emotional exhaustion can weigh heavily. Many leaders feel isolated under the weight of responsibility. These pressures make healthcare leadership one of the most difficult and most important roles of our time.

So why take on this burden? Because it is a sacred privilege. When approached with the right heart, aligned with God's calling, and grounded in the teachings of Jesus, it becomes a purpose-filled vocation. We all long for meaning in our work. This role offers that: the chance to serve, heal, and lead others with hope.

You have the opportunity to shape a culture that honors both caregivers and patients. You can create spaces where people feel seen, supported, and loved, even in a broken system. That kind of leadership reflects the heart of Christ.

As you continue on this journey, remember that courage is not the absence of fear. It is the choice to move forward with faith. Every day you lead with integrity, compassion, and conviction, you live out that courage.

Your calling is sacred. Though the road may be hard, you are never alone. God's strength will sustain you. His Spirit will empower you. And His promise to complete the good work He began in you will remain true. Take heart in this truth and lead boldly, knowing that your efforts matter. Not only in this moment, but in the lives you touch and the legacy you leave behind.

Prayer for Courage and Strength

Lord,
When I feel uncertain or afraid, remind me that You are my strength.
Fill me with courage to do what is right, even when it is hard.
Help me to lead with grace, speak with wisdom, and act with love.
Let Your presence steady me and Your Spirit guide me.
I trust You to carry me through whatever lies ahead.
Amen.

Action Step 1: Pray for Courage Daily

Begin each day with a simple prayer asking God for the courage to lead with wisdom, compassion, and integrity. Invite the Holy Spirit to guide your decisions, especially in moments of uncertainty or fear.

Action Step 2: Identify One Hard but Right Decision

Reflect on a situation where you have been hesitant to act out of fear or discomfort. Ask God for the courage to do what is right, even if it's difficult. Take one step toward resolving it this week.

Action Step 3: Encourage a Fellow Leader or Caregiver

Reach out to someone on your team who may be struggling. Offer a word of encouragement or prayer. Remind them, and yourself, that they are not alone in this work.

Action Step 4: Reconnect with Your Purpose

Take 15 minutes to reflect or journal on why you stepped into healthcare leadership. Revisit the sense of calling that brought you here. Let that clarity renew your sense of purpose and direction.

Reflection and Journal Prompts

1. Where in your leadership right now do you feel the most fear or uncertainty? What might it look like to choose courage in that area?
2. How has God sustained you in past seasons of difficulty or leadership stress? Reflect on a time when you felt overwhelmed but were carried through. What did you learn about God's faithfulness?
3. What does success look like to you as a Christian healthcare leader? Is it aligned with God's definition of faithfulness, or has it been shaped by outside pressures?
4. Who has shown you Christlike courage in leadership? Write about a leader, mentor, or colleague whose courage inspired you. What qualities did they display? How might you embody those same qualities?

Lesson 17

Model the Fruit of the Spirit

Many people struggle to define what it means to be a Christian healthcare leader. Is it about openly expressing faith, or something deeper? While sharing faith can be appropriate in the right context, the most powerful witness often comes through serving others in the character of Jesus. This kind of leadership quietly shapes culture, influences hearts, and reflects faith to those around us.

The Guidance of Scripture

When we consider what this looks like in daily practice, Scripture offers clear guidance. In Galatians 5, Paul explains that the visible evidence of a life aligned with the Holy Spirit is not only a matter of words, but of character. Before introducing the fruit of the Spirit, he contrasts it with what he calls the "acts of the flesh," behaviors such as selfish ambition, discord, envy, outbursts of anger, and other attitudes that fracture community and undermine life-giving leadership. Against this backdrop, Paul offers a vision for the inner life that produces effective, spiritually grounded leadership:

> But the fruit of the Spirit is love, joy, peace, forbearance, kindness, goodness, faithfulness, gentleness and self-control.
>
> Galatians 5:22 (NIV)

In this passage, Paul is not offering a list of optional virtues. He is describing the natural outcome of a life increasingly led, shaped, and

DOI: 10.4324/9781003769781-19

empowered by the Spirit of God. These attributes do more than make someone a "nice leader." They are transformative in environments defined by suffering, complexity, high stakes, and emotional burden, which are the daily realities of healthcare leadership.

Visible Evidence of Spiritual Fruit

As Christians, we can ask what visible evidence of our faith appears in daily life. This fruit includes the character traits described above, but it also takes shape in concrete expressions of compassion, patience, generosity, and service toward others. For healthcare leaders, this can look like:

- Exercising patience in difficult conversations with team members, colleagues, or patients, rather than reacting in frustration.
- Choosing compassion over efficiency when a patient or family needs extra support, even under time pressure.
- Responding to conflict with gentleness and humility, seeking reconciliation rather than escalation.
- Maintaining self-control during stressful moments, remaining calm and grounded when emotions run high.
- Making decisions with integrity, even when no one is watching and easier shortcuts are available.
- Leading with kindness in feedback and accountability, communicating with truth and respect rather than harshness.
- Demonstrating faithfulness in commitments by consistently following through on responsibilities, promises, and care standards.
- Creating an atmosphere of peace within your team by fostering collaboration, respect, and stability instead of anxiety or division.
- Practicing joy in leadership by bringing encouragement, gratitude, and hope into the workplace.

Spiritual fruit grows more evident when we regularly examine our decisions and actions in light of Paul's teaching. By practicing these traits intentionally and reflecting on daily interactions, we cultivate a leadership style that is not only effective but visibly grounded in faith. The fruit we bear is more than personal virtue. It serves as a witness to others, shaping culture, strengthening relationships, and demonstrating the transformative power of a life aligned with God's Spirit.

Remaining Rooted in Christ

True and lasting spiritual fruit originates from our relationship with Christ. Jesus clarifies its source:

> I am the vine; you are the branches. If you remain in me and I in you, you will bear much fruit; apart from me you can do nothing.
>
> John 15:5 (NIV)

This passage reminds us that Christ must remain at the center of our lives for good fruit to grow. We are not alone in this work, nor are we expected to lead by our own strength. As we invite God into our leadership and maintain an ongoing, prayerful relationship with Him, the Holy Spirit equips and empowers us to live and lead in these ways.

When we draw close to God through prayer and reliance on His strength, we experience His peace in tangible ways. The Spirit shapes our responses, making us more likely to act with compassion, love, grace, and humility. When we drift from God and rely on our own strength, that sense of His presence diminishes, and our leadership reflects it.

The Ripple Effect of Fruitful Leadership

One of the beautiful realities of the fruit of the Spirit is that its impact extends beyond ourselves. As the Spirit cultivates this fruit in our lives, others notice the transformation in our words, actions, and decisions. Over time, this quiet faithfulness shapes culture and creates a ripple effect that extends far beyond a single role or moment.

Ultimately, modeling the fruit of the Spirit is more than a personal discipline. It is a form of ministry. Each act of patience, kindness, or integrity has the potential to encourage, heal, and reshape the environments around us. As Christian healthcare leaders, our calling is to lead in ways that reflect Christ, allowing His Spirit to bear fruit through us so that the world we serve becomes more compassionate, just, and whole. When we lead with the Spirit's fruit, we do more than guide teams or organizations. We reflect Christ each day to a world deeply in need of His love.

Action Step 1: Pause and Reflect Daily

Take 5–10 minutes each day to review your interactions and decisions. Identify moments where you acted with love, patience, or integrity, and areas where the Spirit's fruit could have been more evident.

Action Step 2: Choose One Fruit to Focus On

Each week, select one aspect of the Spirit's fruit (e.g., gentleness, joy, or self-control) and intentionally practice it in your leadership interactions.

Action Step 3: Invite Feedback from Your Team

Ask trusted colleagues or team members how your words and actions reflect the Spirit's fruit. Use their observations to guide personal growth and leadership adjustments.

Action Step 4: Leadership in Prayer

Begin each day or shift with a brief prayer, inviting the Holy Spirit to guide your decisions, shape your responses, and help you demonstrate Christlike character in all interactions.

Reflection and Journal Prompts

1. Reflect on today's interactions. In which moments did I demonstrate patience, kindness, or integrity? Where did I rely on my own strength rather than the Spirit?
2. Which aspect of the fruit of the Spirit do I most need to cultivate in my leadership right now, and why? How might focusing on this fruit change my interactions with my team or those we serve?

3. How have my words and actions influenced the culture of my team or organization recently? What evidence do I see that Spirit-led leadership impacts others beyond myself?
4. How can I intentionally draw closer to Jesus this week in order to bear more spiritual fruit? What specific practices (prayer, reflection, Scripture, mentoring) will help me stay rooted in Him?

Lesson 18

Develop Self-Control

Few things are as challenging as maintaining emotional self-control in the face of anger, fear, or frustration. Yet for Christian healthcare leaders, this discipline is essential in both leadership and daily life. None of us are perfect. But with practical tools, intentional reflection, and consistent practice, we can gradually respond in a more Christlike manner. Developing self-control is less about perfection and more about progress, taking steps each day to align our actions with our values, even in stressful moments.

This may require consistent effort, especially given the nature of healthcare organizations. It is not a sign of moral failure but a reflection of our humanity. Healthcare professionals often work within systems that are stressful, fast-paced, and at times dysfunctional. These conditions rarely bring out the best in people. Yet personal, professional, and spiritual growth is possible when we implement practices that help us respond with intention rather than impulse.

Daily Practices to Cultivate Self-Control

Daily practices that help cultivate self-control include:

- **Pause before responding**
  Take slow, deep breaths or silently count to ten before speaking in stressful situations. This allows emotions to settle and reason to catch up with reaction.

DOI: 10.4324/9781003769781-20

- **Pray in the moment**
  Offer a brief internal prayer, such as "Lord, please let me feel your peace and presence," before responding to conflict, anger, or pressure.
- **Reflect daily**
  Review your interactions, attitudes, and responses at the end of each day. Ask, "Where did I show self-control today, and where do I need growth?"
- **Seek accountability**
  Invite a trusted colleague, mentor, or spiritual friend to check in periodically and offer honest encouragement and feedback.
- **Practice scriptural grounding**
  Memorize verses that reinforce patience, gentleness, and self-control so they come to mind naturally in challenging moments.
- **Respond to the problem, not the emotion**
  Focus on the actual issue rather than the feelings driving your reaction. For example, if a nurse snaps in frustration, address the workload or support needed instead of reacting to the tone.
- **Reframe the moment**
  Recognize that anger, anxiety, and frustration are signals, not commands. They inform your feelings but do not have to dictate your actions.
- **Practice empathy before responding**
  Pause to consider what the other person may be experiencing beneath their words or behavior. Empathy does not excuse poor conduct, but it helps you respond with calm, clarity, and self-control rather than reaction.
- **Practice guided meditation before difficult interactions**
  Set aside 20 minutes before meetings or conversations where conflict is likely and engage in a guided meditation or visualization. This helps calm your body, regulate your nervous system, and respond with clarity rather than stress.
- **Establish twice-daily meditation sessions**
  Incorporate brief morning and evening meditation sessions into your routine. These practices reduce accumulated stress and cultivate a calm, centered state of mind.
- **Spend time in prayer ahead of challenges**
  Before difficult situations, pray for the strength and grace to remain calm and reflect God's character in your words, attitude, and decisions.
- **Prioritize physical well-being**
  Daily movement and exposure to nature support mental health, reduce stress, and help regulate emotions. Even short walks, stretching, or time outdoors can improve composure and focus.

- **Identify triggers and plan responses**
Reflect on your emotional triggers and decide how you will respond in advance. Mastering this proactive approach is more effective than relying on willpower in the moment.

Neuroscience and Formation

My personal approach includes 20-minute meditations in the morning and evening, regular exercise, time in sunshine and nature, and a brief meditation or prayer before meetings where conflict is likely. Practiced consistently, this routine has been transformative.

Modern neuroscience supports these practices, showing that repetition reshapes the brain over time. Techniques such as meditation, deep breathing, and daily reflection create new neural pathways that make calm, thoughtful responses more automatic. Other mindfulness and stress reduction practices to consider include:

- **Journaling**
Writing down thoughts, stressors, or emotions helps process experiences, identify triggers, and track growth.
- **Deep-breathing or box-breathing exercises**
Simple, structured breathing practices can calm the nervous system anywhere.
- **Gratitude practice**
Taking a few minutes each day to note things you are thankful for shifts perspective, reduces anxiety, and promotes emotional resilience.
- **Mindful breaks during the day**
Short pauses, such as stepping away from screens, stretching, or noticing your surroundings, help prevent burnout and maintain focus.
- **Sleep hygiene**
Regular, adequate sleep is foundational for emotional regulation and stress resilience.
- **Healthy social support**
Maintaining relationships with friends, mentors, or peers provides emotional outlets and accountability.
- **Limiting overstimulation**
Reducing multitasking, screen time, or exposure to negative media can help maintain mental clarity and composure.

- **Healthy diet**
  Balanced meals, adequate hydration, and limiting caffeine, processed foods, and excess sugar support energy, mood, and emotional resilience. Caring for the body strengthens the ability to maintain calm, focus, and self-control under pressure.

The Power of a Steady Presence

It is easy to assume that the most peaceful and composed leaders are simply born with this ability. Yet they are human too. In most cases, their calm presence is the result of healthy coping mechanisms and regular practices that help them maintain emotional steadiness.

As I often say, the best leaders are like the calm at the center of the storm. This quality, more than many others, draws people to them. It creates a sense of safety, trust, and stability even in challenging circumstances. These are the leaders we long to work for, and with intentional practice, you can become this kind of leader as well.

Grounding Self-Control in Scripture

Our ability to remain calm, centered, and Christlike under pressure is not just a leadership skill. It is deeply supported by Scripture:

> Everyone should be quick to listen, slow to speak and slow to become angry, because human anger does not produce the righteousness that God desires.
>
> James 1:19–20 (NIV)

This verse highlights the importance of deliberate restraint in our words and emotions, emphasizing that true righteousness flows from measured, thoughtful responses rather than anger. For leaders, cultivating self-control is not merely a professional habit. It is a spiritual practice that honors God and models His character to those around us. Another verse reinforces this guidance, reminding us to release anxiety, pray, and invite God's peace into our lives:

> Do not be anxious about anything, but in every situation, by prayer and petition, with thanksgiving, present your requests to God. And

the peace of God, which transcends all understanding, will guard your hearts and your minds in Christ Jesus.

Philippians 4:6–7 (NIV)

The Reward of Practice

Once you know practical ways to develop self-control, the next step is to practice them. Like any skill, your ability to respond well will grow over time. How much it develops depends on your commitment, because this work is not easy. It requires making self-control a continuous priority.

Yet the effort is worth it. As you cultivate calm, centered, Christlike responses, you will notice the impact not only on your own peace of mind but also on your relationships, your team, and the culture around you. Over time, what once felt difficult can become a steady, stabilizing presence that others rely on and admire.

Action Step 1: Choose One Practice to Implement Daily

Select one self-control practice, such as pausing before responding, a brief morning prayer, or a short meditation, and commit to doing it every day for the next two weeks.

Action Step 2: Identify Your Triggers

Write down the top 3 situations or behaviors that most often trigger reactive responses in you. Reflect on why they affect you and plan how you will respond differently next time.

Action Step 3: Schedule Reflection Time

Set aside 10 minutes at the end of each day to evaluate your emotional responses. Ask: *Where did I demonstrate self-control today? Where do I need growth?* Track this progress in a journal.

Action Step 4: Ask for Accountability

Invite one trusted colleague, mentor, or spiritual friend to check in with you periodically about your self-control goals, giving permission for honest feedback and encouragement.

Journal and Reflection Prompts

1. Where did I face moments today that tested my self-control, and how did I respond? Did I react impulsively, or did I pause and respond with intention? What influenced my behavior?
2. What emotions showed up most strongly for me today, and what were they trying to tell me? Reflect on what your emotions revealed about your inner state such as stress, fear, fatigue, frustration, or something else.
3. In which moments today did I sense God's presence or miss the opportunity to invite Him in? How did prayer, Scripture, or spiritual grounding shape (or fail to shape) your responses?
4. What one small change can I make tomorrow that would strengthen my ability to remain calm, centered, and Christlike under pressure? Focus on a specific, realistic adjustment, such as pausing before responding, preparing through prayer, or taking a short mindful break.

Lesson 19

Start and End Every Day with Prayer

Developing a consistent pattern of prayer is like building any other discipline. At first, it can feel challenging, but with repetition it becomes second nature. Prayer is one of the most important practices for maintaining spiritual health. It has the power to shape our days, influence our leadership, and center our lives around God's presence rather than our circumstances.

Many believers draw close to God in times of uncertainty, pain, or fear. Yet when life improves, prayer often becomes shorter, less frequent, and less intentional. This is important to recognize, because we need God just as much in seasons of stability as in times of crisis. Many of us cling to Him in moments of fear, only to breathe a sigh of relief when He answers, then slowly drift until the next storm arrives.

As healthcare leaders, the storms rarely stay away for long. In fact, they often arrive daily. This reality can feel like a blessing or a burden, depending on how we frame it. Constant pressure reminds us of our need for God's peace, strength, and guidance. At the same time, no one is designed to carry unrelenting stress without serious consequences for mind, body, and spirit.

In settings like this, regular prayer is not just a spiritual discipline. It is a lifeline. When the waves rise and you feel close to going under, prayer can keep you afloat. It also reminds us that as faith-filled leaders, we do not

DOI: 10.4324/9781003769781-21

have to rely solely on our own strength. This truth can be transformational when fully internalized in our thoughts, habits, and daily actions.

If you have walked through difficult seasons, you may already know this. In those moments, God's presence can be life-changing, even life-saving. When that sense of presence begins to fade, it can feel like something is deeply missing. The good news is that life does not have to be lived in cycles of spiritual connection and disconnect.

Practical Prayer Routines

Morning prayer may include gratitude and requests for guidance, strength, and clarity. Evening prayer may include reflection, confession, thanksgiving, and surrender of the day's concerns. You can share anything with God as you would with a trusted friend. The key is consistency, not length. You do not need a rigid structure. Instead, consider a few simple patterns like those below.

Morning 5-Minute Routine

- **Minute 1–2.** Begin with gratitude. Thank God for a new day, your health, your team, and opportunities to serve.
- **Minute 2–3.** Ask for guidance. Pray for clarity, wisdom, and patience in your decisions and interactions today.
- **Minute 3–4.** Offer your schedule. Entrust meetings, patient encounters, and responsibilities to God.
- **Minute 4–5.** Center yourself. Take a few deep breaths, focus silently on God's presence, and commit to noticing His guidance throughout the day.

Breath Prayer (for Moments throughout the Day)

- Choose a short phrase such as: *"Lord, please guide me"* or *"Be with me today."*
- **Inhale** silently with the first word, **exhale** with the second.
- Repeat for 1–3 minutes to refocus and reconnect with God's presence.

Evening Prayer and Reflection (5–10 Minutes)

- **Minute 1–2.** Thank God for today and notice blessings, growth, or answered prayer.
- **Minute 2–4.** Reflect on challenges you faced and areas to surrender to God.
- **Minute 4–6.** Seek forgiveness or release. Let go of frustrations, worries, or mistakes.
- **Minute 6–8.** Pray for others, including staff, patients, family, and those in need.
- **Minute 8–10.** Center and rest. Take a few deep breaths, visualizing God's peace filling your mind and body before sleep.

Journal Integration

To deepen your reflection, consider keeping a small notebook. Spend 1–2 minutes writing:

- A blessing you noticed today.
- A moment where you sensed God's guidance.
- One area you want to entrust to Him tomorrow.

Prayer as a Conversation, Not a Checklist

These examples are simply guides. The goal is not to "complete" a prayer routine but to relate to God in a genuine and ongoing way. Prayer becomes richer when we:

- Move from formal recitation to real dialogue with God throughout the day.
- Include brief moments of silence, listening, or Scripture meditation during natural breaks.
- Recognize prayer opportunities in small daily moments such as patient rounds, decision-making, or commuting.

Overcoming Obstacles to Consistent Prayer

Even with sincere commitment, maintaining a consistent prayer life can be difficult. Common obstacles include fatigue, distraction, time pressure, or feeling distant from God. Practical tools such as reminders, journaling, or pairing prayer with existing routines can help sustain the practice. Most importantly, extend grace to yourself when you fall short. Spiritual discipline grows through encouragement, not self-criticism.

Integrating Prayer with Leadership

Prayer can be woven naturally into leadership. This may mean praying regularly for your team, bringing decisions to God, or using prayer as a healthy outlet for personal stress. In faith-based environments, it may also include visible practices such as opening meetings in prayer or pausing to pray with staff during difficult moments. In my own leadership journey, I served in several faith-based healthcare organizations where prayer became part of the organizational rhythm. During seasons of stress, loss, or fear, these practices became even more vital.

Loss is an unavoidable reality in healthcare, and in long-term care settings, it can be especially personal. As a licensed nursing home administrator, I experienced firsthand the deep bonds that form between residents, staff, and leadership. When someone passes away, it can feel like losing a member of the family. The emotional weight often falls heavily on frontline caregivers such as nursing assistants, nurses, therapists, and others who shared daily life with that person. When leaders pause to pray with their teams in these moments, it can make a profound difference. Prayer acknowledges shared grief, invites God's presence into the room, and reminds everyone that they do not carry their losses alone.

Leading as a Christian in Healthcare

This is one of the defining distinctions between faith-based leadership and leadership without a spiritual foundation. What does it mean to lead as a Christian in healthcare? At its core, it means inviting God into the moments that matter most, joyful and heartbreaking alike, and anchoring hope not only in human strength but in the promises of Christ.

Christian leaders are not called to have every answer. They are called to continually point themselves and others back to the One who does. As you lead, remember that your reliance on God not only sustains you, but also inspires those around you to place their trust in Him.

Action Step 1: Schedule Your Prayer Times

Identify a consistent time in the morning and evening to pray, even if it's just five minutes. Treat it as an unmissable appointment with God.

Action Step 2: Practice Brief "Breath Prayers" Throughout the Day

Use short phrases like "Lord, guide me" during transitions, patient rounds, or stressful moments to stay connected to God continuously.

Action Step 3: Incorporate Reflection or Journaling

Each evening, write down at least one blessing, one challenge where you sensed God's guidance, and one concern you want to entrust to Him tomorrow.

Action Step 4: Pray with and for Your Team

Make it a habit to pause and pray during moments of stress, loss, or celebration. Model faith-filled leadership by inviting God into daily workplace realities.

Reflection and Journal Prompts

1. Take a few minutes to write down three specific things you are grateful for this morning, big or small. Then reflect on how you can intentionally invite God into your schedule, interactions, and mindset

today. Consider: How might beginning my day with prayer shape my attitude and choices?

2. Reflect on one decision, meeting, or patient interaction that may require wisdom or patience today. Write down how you plan to invite God into that situation. Consider: What fears, biases, or assumptions might I need to surrender in order to respond in alignment with God's guidance?
3. At the end of the day, journal about moments where you sensed God's presence and moments where you felt distant. Identify any frustrations, worries, or mistakes and intentionally surrender them to God in writing. Consider: How can releasing control to God bring peace and clarity for tomorrow?
4. Reflect on the people you lead, serve, or care for, including staff, patients, or family members. Write down specific prayer points for them, noting both their needs and your own role in supporting them. Consider: How can my prayers for others shape the culture, compassion, and spiritual tone of my leadership?

Lesson 20

Stand Firm When Faith Is Tested

As Christian healthcare leaders, there will be seasons when our faith is stretched, strained, or even shaken. Challenges arise that test not only our skills but also our character, convictions, and trust in God. Whether it is the weight of organizational pressure, difficult decisions that affect people's lives, or personal trials behind the scenes, we must learn to stand firm when the ground beneath us feels unsteady.

Scripture does not promise that we will avoid trials, but it does promise that God will strengthen, uphold, and refine us through them. In these moments, our leadership becomes more than a position. It becomes a testimony. When we stand firm in faith, we show that our trust is in God, not in the shifting circumstances around us. The key in these moments is choosing trust over fear and allowing challenges to refine our character. As Scripture reminds us:

> Blessed is the one who perseveres under trial because, having stood the test, that person will receive the crown of life that the Lord has promised to those who love him.
>
> James 1:12 (NIV)

During such seasons, we have two choices. We can either pull away from God and rely on our own strength and wisdom, or we can cling more deeply to Him, asking for the strength, protection, and guidance needed to

DOI: 10.4324/9781003769781-22

move forward. Christians have relied on this protection for centuries, and Scripture gives us clear direction and encouragement:

> Therefore put on the full armor of God, so that when the day of evil comes, you may be able to stand your ground, and after you have done everything, to stand.
>
> Ephesians 6:13 (NIV)

A Story of Faith in the Fire

Healthcare leadership today can feel like stepping into a fiery furnace. I experienced this in many ways over the years. In senior leadership, challenges often come from every direction at once. The pressures are heavy, the stakes are high, and the challenges can be both professional and personal.

At times, I faced criticism, misunderstanding, and even direct threats based on decisions I believed were right and necessary. These challenges can come from staff, patients, family members, attorneys, surveyors, board members, and others. When the stress is intense and the heat rises, it is easy to feel alone, vulnerable, or overwhelmed. Yet in these moments, when our faith is tested, it has the chance to shine most brightly.

If you are going through something like this right now, remember: even the most successful leaders do not escape criticism, threats, or hardship. Most do not share these struggles publicly, and they rarely appear on LinkedIn highlight reels. But trials are part of leadership, and many have walked this path before you.

Faith-based leaders strive to lead with morality, integrity, and empathy. They seek team members who share these values and allow them to guide decisions. Yet trials are inevitable. Sometimes they may even feel designed to bring strong leaders down. Always remember, however, that God is your refuge and a strong fortress in times of trouble. With Him by your side, you can stand firm, confident, and empowered to persevere.

Biblical Example: Faith in the Fire

In Daniel 3, King Nebuchadnezzar commanded everyone to bow to a golden image. Shadrach, Meshach, and Abednego refused because of their loyalty to God. Furious, the king had them thrown into a blazing furnace heated seven times hotter than usual.

Even in the furnace, God was with them. Not a hair on their heads was singed, and they emerged completely unharmed. Their unwavering faith under extreme pressure was a powerful testimony, showing that God's presence can sustain us even in the most impossible circumstances.

For leaders in healthcare, and in any high-pressure role, there will be moments that feel like walking into a furnace. There will be decisions that invite criticism, crises that seem overwhelming, and trials that test our character. In these moments, our calling is to stand firm in faith, trusting that God is with us.

Standing Firm in the Fire

Standing firm in faith does not always remove the fire, but it does assure us of God's presence within it. That presence makes all the difference in how we lead, respond, and endure. As healthcare leaders, we are called to model this truth for others by embodying courage, integrity, and trust in God. Now more than ever, healthcare workers need leaders who remain steady under pressure, make decisions with conviction, treat others with empathy, and inspire confidence even in the most challenging circumstances.

By standing firm in faith, we not only navigate our own trials with strength but also create an environment in which others feel empowered to do the same. In every high-pressure situation, we can choose trust over fear, obedience over compromise, and hope over despair. In doing so, we demonstrate that true leadership is rooted not in position or power, but in unwavering faith and reliance on God.

Action Step 1: Daily Armor Check

Begin each day by mentally "putting on" the full armor of God (Ephesians 6:10–18). Reflect on each piece, including truth, righteousness, peace, faith, salvation, and the Word, and consider how it applies to the challenges you may face that day. This primes your heart and mind to respond from faith rather than fear.

Action Step 2: Anchor in Scripture

Identify two to three key verses that speak to perseverance, trust, or God's protection (e.g., James 1:12, Isaiah 41:10). Write them down, memorize them, or keep them visible at your workspace. When trials arise, repeat these promises to yourself to anchor your faith in God's truth.

Action Step 3: Reflect and Journal

After difficult moments, take 5–10 minutes to journal about what you experienced, how you responded, and where God was present. Note areas where fear tried to take hold and how faith helped you stand firm. Over time, this builds awareness and strengthens resilience.

Action Step 4: Seek Faithful Support

Identify a small circle of trusted colleagues, mentors, or spiritual advisors who can pray with you, offer encouragement, and hold you accountable. Share challenges openly, seek guidance, and allow their support to reinforce your steadfastness in difficult times.

Reflection and Journal Prompts

1. What current challenges or pressures in your leadership feel like a "fiery furnace"? How are these situations testing your faith, character, or patience?
2. In moments of pressure, where have you relied on your own strength instead of trusting God? How could choosing faith over fear change your response?
3. Reflect on a past trial where you experienced God's presence or guidance. What did you learn about His faithfulness, and how can that encourage you in your current situation?
4. How can your steadfastness in faith influence your team, patients, or colleagues? What specific actions could you take to model trust, courage, and integrity under pressure?

III

LEADING WITH PRESENCE AND COMPASSION

Lesson 21

Sow Seeds of Kindness

This lesson explores the importance of small acts of kindness in shaping the culture of healthcare organizations. As a Christian healthcare leader, you may not be able to fix the entire system, but you can create a micro-culture of kindness, compassion, and hope wherever you serve. You may have read leadership advice about celebrating small wins, but as Christians, we are called to define success by a deeper standard. Acts of kindness are victories we can celebrate every day. Always remember: kindness is not just a virtue. It is a way of being. Small actions ripple outward, touching both the patients we serve and the colleagues who work alongside us. Over time, these acts can transform entire communities.

A Lesson in Kindness

Early in my career, I learned the quiet yet profound influence of kindness firsthand. I was working in mental health as a children's case manager in an inner-city middle school. One day, a teacher snapped at me in a way that felt sharp and hurtful. Later that evening, while walking through a grocery store, I noticed a small holiday coffee mug filled with chocolates and a simple decoration. On impulse, I bought it and decided to give it to her the next day.

The following morning, she met me with her usual unfriendly stare, until she saw what I was holding. Her expression softened. I said, "I thought you might have had a hard day yesterday, so I brought you this." In an instant, everything shifted. Tears welled in her eyes, and it was as if a different

DOI: 10.4324/9781003769781-24

person, someone softer and hidden beneath the surface, appeared before me. That small gesture became the beginning of a genuine and lasting friendship.

This experience has stayed with me. It reminds me that the person we see in a difficult moment is rarely the whole story. There is almost always someone inside, longing to be seen, understood, and treated gently. As leaders, we have the privilege of helping that person emerge through kindness in our actions and grace in our words.

Leading with Kindness

Who will you help today? Start with your leadership team and frontline caregivers. Then look for small, meaningful acts of kindness that ripple through your organization. These actions are contagious. Just as emotions spread in groups, so does compassion. The behavior of leaders is especially powerful. It is always being observed and often repeated.

It doesn't have to be a grand gesture. It can be a quiet word of encouragement, a moment of presence, or a prayer whispered over a colleague's burden. When kindness becomes intentional, it becomes part of the culture.

Consider what it would look like to make kindness a visible, shared value in your organization. Not just encouraged but modeled, celebrated, and woven into the rhythms of leadership. You may even formalize it by naming kindness as a core value and identifying the daily behaviors that express it.

Making Kindness Visible

- Start meetings with a moment of gratitude or a word of encouragement.
- Celebrate small wins publicly, especially those involving compassion.
- Include kindness in leadership competencies and evaluations.
- Create a "kindness wall" where staff can post moments they've witnessed.
- Send handwritten notes of thanks or affirmation to staff.
- Share stories that highlight both clinical excellence and human care.
- Model calm, grace-filled responses in high-stress situations.

Even one or two consistent practices can change the emotional and spiritual tone of your team. When kindness is made visible and repeatable, it becomes part of your culture. Scripture affirms this calling clearly:

> Be kind and compassionate to one another, forgiving each other, just as in Christ God forgave you.
>
> Ephesians 4:32 (NIV)

This is not just encouragement. It is a command rooted in Christ's own example. It sets a standard for how we treat others, not only with professional respect, but with spiritual love.

Of course, not everyone sees kindness as strength. In some leadership circles, it is dismissed as weakness or sentimentality. But true strength is often quiet and unseen. It is the strength to resist anger when the system feels broken, the grace to offer compassion when you're stretched thin, the courage to lead with mercy, not force, the wisdom to model gentleness, not just grit, and the heart to sow kindness, alongside competence.

By honoring these acts as small wins, you are modeling the leadership of Jesus Himself. Just as Christ, the Good Shepherd, carefully tends His flock, you too can tend those under your care with kindness, compassion, and courage. Kindness is not weakness. It is quiet strength in action. The kind that reflects Christ and transforms culture, one relationship at a time. This is the work of leadership. This is the way of Jesus.

Prayer for a Kind Heart

Lord Jesus,
You are the Good Shepherd, full of compassion and mercy.
Teach me to lead with kindness, even in small and quiet ways.
Help me to see every person I encounter as someone You dearly love.
Give me the strength to be gentle,
the courage to be compassionate,
and the wisdom to sow seeds of kindness wherever I go.
May my leadership reflect Your love,
and may these small acts of grace grow into a culture of healing
and hope.
In Your holy name I pray,
Amen.

Action Step 1: Identify and Affirm Acts of Kindness Daily

Look for one small act of kindness in your team each day, and name it out loud.

Action Step 2: Model Kindness in Leadership Conversations

Start meetings or difficult discussions with a word of grace, gratitude, or encouragement.

Action Step 3: Make Kindness a Shared Value

Invite your team to define what kindness looks like in practice. Then, choose one way to make it visible.

Action Step 4: Anchor Kindness in Scripture

Memorize Ephesians 4:32 or display it in a visible space. Let it serve as a daily reminder of the kind of leader you are called to be.

Reflection and Journal Prompts

1. When was the last time someone showed you unexpected kindness at work? How did it affect your mindset, motivation, or sense of connection?
2. In what ways have you seen kindness (or a lack of it) shape the culture of your organization?
3. Are there any moments this week when you missed an opportunity to respond with kindness? What held you back?
4. Read and reflect on Ephesians 4:32. What part of this verse speaks to you most: kindness, compassion, forgiveness? How can you embody this more fully in your leadership?

Lesson 22

Lead by Listening

When you think of leadership, what images come to mind? Perhaps a confident individual directing and guiding a team, or a leader casting a bold vision for others to follow. But consider a different picture: a quiet, humble leader who listens to understand rather than simply respond. A leader who builds trust, welcomes wisdom, and speaks only after listening deeply. As Christian healthcare leaders, we are called to this kind of attentive presence. When we listen first to God and then to others, we create space for reflection and discernment, even amid the noise and urgency of healthcare.

I once heard someone refer to this constant pressure as the *tyranny of today*. That phrase stayed with me because it captures how immediate demands can crowd out deeper listening. Emails flood our inboxes, crises arise without warning, and urgent decisions press in from every direction. Yet listening remains a choice. We can choose to slow down, set aside distractions, and be fully present. The space between breaths is sacred. When we take time to truly listen, we reflect Christ in both our actions and our decisions. As Scripture reminds us:

> Everyone should be quick to listen, slow to speak and slow to become angry.
>
> James 1:19 (NIV)

This verse captures the heart of faithful leadership. Listening before responding requires humility, patience, and restraint. It is not always easy, especially in executive roles where decisions must be made regularly and

DOI: 10.4324/9781003769781-25

often under pressure. Yet how we listen, or fail to listen, shapes the culture we create, one conversation at a time.

Start with God First

Listening deeply to others becomes much easier when we first learn to listen deeply to God. We have already discussed the importance of regular prayer, yet prayer can easily become one-sided. We speak, share our burdens, ask for guidance, and then move on with the day. But how often do we sit in silence afterward and truly listen for His response? Consider this passage from 1 Kings:

> The Lord said, 'Go out and stand on the mountain in the presence of the Lord, for the Lord is about to pass by.' Then a great and powerful wind tore the mountains apart and shattered the rocks before the Lord, but the Lord was not in the wind. After the wind there was an earthquake, but the Lord was not in the earthquake. After the earthquake came a fire, but the Lord was not in the fire. And after the fire came a gentle whisper. When Elijah heard it, he pulled his cloak over his face and went out and stood at the mouth of the cave.
>
> 1 Kings 19:11–12 (NIV)

God was not in the wind, the earthquake, or the fire, but in the gentle whisper. This passage reminds us of the importance of creating space for silence, stillness, and attentive listening, even in the midst of chaos. We need intentional moments of quiet that allow us to hear what God has for us. As we practice patience and silence, we develop the discipline of listening deeply. Over time, this practice reshapes how we listen, not only to God, but also to one another. When we learn to listen well in our personal walk with God and in one-to-one relationships, we can begin to weave this posture of listening into the culture of our organizations.

A Listening Culture

It is one thing to practice deep listening personally, and another to embed it into the culture of an organization. This work begins by grounding the value of listening in mission, formation, and values statements and then identifying practical behaviors that demonstrate what listening looks like in daily practice. When listening is formalized in this way, it becomes a foundation for decision-making, leadership development, training, and evaluation. It also shapes strategic conversations at the board level and influences every layer of the organization.

Values and belief statements are powerful because they are meant to be lived. They should be practical, concrete, and measurable, defining how people treat one another throughout the organization. When done well, they allow staff to hold leadership accountable. Good intentions alone are not enough. Without structural reinforcement, it is easy to drift back into the tyranny of today. Clear expectations help leaders and teams return to the right priorities when pressure threatens to pull them off course.

This priority becomes especially important during times of organizational change, when full stakeholder inclusion and hearing every voice becomes essential. One tool I found particularly valuable in my own leadership journey was the use of structured learning circles in small-group meetings. In these sessions, each participant is given dedicated time to speak while others listen with full attention. This stands in contrast to typical meetings dominated by a single authority figure assumed to be the expert. A facilitator still guides the process, but leadership becomes collaborative rather than controlling. Other ways leaders can integrate listening into organizational culture include:

- Beginning meetings with a moment of silence to allow people to settle their minds and listen before speaking
- Building structured time into agendas so that every voice is heard, not only the loudest or the most senior
- Training managers in active listening skills such as reflective listening, summarizing, and asking clarifying questions before responding
- Creating leadership rounding practices in which leaders ask open, unhurried questions and truly listen to front-line staff
- Encouraging teams to pause before major decisions and ask, "What are we not hearing yet?"
- Inviting staff feedback anonymously and visibly demonstrating how that feedback has shaped decisions
- Holding regular listening sessions or town halls where the primary goal is understanding others rather than presenting information
- Including listening as a leadership competency in evaluations, giving it measurable organizational weight

- Providing protected time for prayer, reflection, Sabbath rest, or spiritual renewal for staff who desire it
- Modeling listening at the top, with leaders who slow down, resist jumping to conclusions, and demonstrate that thoughtful consideration is valued more than speed

Listening with Wisdom and Limits

While these practices can meaningfully strengthen organizational culture, they must be implemented with wisdom. In my own experience, I once required every leader in the organization to round quarterly with each person who reported to them. On the surface, this expectation seemed reasonable and aligned with our values. As a CEO, I had a manageable number of direct reports and already met weekly with each of them, so the requirement was not burdensome for me. But for others, especially those in nursing leadership, it quickly became overwhelming.

In our senior living community, we had hundreds of team members. Nurse leaders were already working long hours, filling shifts due to workforce shortages, responding to surveyor complaint visits, managing regulatory surveys, addressing staff and family concerns, and navigating increasing documentation demands. At the same time, we were undergoing significant organizational transformation toward person-centered care and a physical renovation to create a more homelike environment. Change of this magnitude requires deep listening, and rounding was one of the tools we used. But it also added pressure to leaders who were already stretched thin. As a result, it created an unsustainable workload, reduced morale, and harmed trust in senior leadership.

This reality is common in healthcare today. Many leaders are asked to carry more and more until they are operating near a breaking point. Wise senior leaders recognize this and engage their management teams in honest conversations before rolling out new expectations. They ask whether a practice is feasible, explore what support is needed, and consider how responsibilities might be balanced or adjusted. Sometimes the conclusion is that an initiative is valuable but not sustainable in its current form. Even with the best intentions, systems must begin by modeling the discipline they promote. The first step in building a listening culture is to listen.

Practice What You Preach

When we practice deep listening consistently, our presence changes. We become slower to react and quicker to understand. People begin to feel seen rather than supervised, valued rather than managed, included rather than overlooked. Over time, culture shifts, one relationship, one decision, and one conversation at a time.

We may not be able to transform the entire healthcare system, but we can shape the environments we lead. And the character of those environments will often reflect the character of our own inner life and our relationship with God. A listening leader creates a listening culture. A listening culture reflects a listening faith. And when we lead in a posture that is quiet, attentive, patient, and open, we embody the leadership of Christ in a world that deeply needs His presence.

Action Step 1: Start Your Day with Listening Prayer

Set aside at least five minutes each morning not only to speak to God, but to sit quietly, breathe, and listen. Ask, "Lord, what do You want me to hear today?"

Action Step 2: Practice One Listening Habit in Every Conversation

Before responding, pause long enough to fully understand. Ask one clarifying question or reflect back what you heard to ensure mutual understanding.

Action Step 3: Create One Space for Listening Each Week

Choose a practical rhythm such as a weekly listening circle, open office hour, reflective huddle, or leadership rounding, and protect this time as sacred, unhurried listening.

Action Step 4: Evaluate One Decision Through a Listening Lens

Before approving a policy, initiative, or major change, ask yourself and your team, “Whose voice is missing, and what do we need to hear before moving forward?”

Reflection and Journal Prompts

1. Reflect on a recent conversation where you felt rushed or distracted. How might your response have changed if you had paused to listen more deeply? What would listening to God first have looked like in that moment?
2. Who on your team or in your organization do you rarely hear from? How can you create intentional space to listen to their perspective this week?
3. Consider one aspect of your organization’s culture that discourages deep listening (e.g., rushed meetings, hierarchy, constant crises). What small, practical steps could you take to counteract it?
4. Reflect on a “gentle whisper” moment in your own life, when God spoke quietly amid the noise. How can you cultivate more of these moments daily, and how would they influence your leadership?

Lesson 23

Build Trust Consistently

Both personally and professionally, the strongest relationships are built on trust. It takes time to develop, and once broken, it can be difficult to restore. For that reason, we should treat trust as something precious from the beginning of every relationship.

As leaders, we can do this with each team member. When we consistently demonstrate behaviors that build trust with individuals, we help them do the same with one another. Over time, this creates a ripple effect throughout the organization.

Trust also shapes organizational culture when it is embedded in values and belief statements and reinforced through observable, coachable behaviors expected of all team members. Ideally, these behaviors should be concrete, simple, and easy to understand. But how should we determine them, and where should they be rooted? Ultimately, they should be grounded in the life and teachings of Jesus.

For Christians, trust grows when our words and actions align with Christlike integrity. This includes reliability, honesty, transparency, kindness, emotional intelligence, and character. Perhaps most important is how we make people feel and how we treat them, especially in difficult moments, with safety, respect, and grace.

Trusting God, Trusting Ourselves

Before we can consistently build trust with others, we must reflect inward. Do you believe you are worthy of trust? Can you acknowledge

DOI: 10.4324/9781003769781-26

past mistakes while also trusting yourself to walk in integrity moving forward? For many of us, forgiving others comes more easily than forgiving ourselves. Yet holding on to guilt can be deeply counterproductive.

It is important to recognize where we have fallen short. Even better is seeking God's forgiveness and asking for the strength to grow and do better in the future. Then comes the hardest part: accepting that forgiveness and truly letting it go. Only from that place can we move forward with renewed confidence and a firm commitment to lead with integrity.

Trusting ourselves from that point forward requires acting with integrity in all matters, big and small. It also means understanding that, even if no one else knows, God knows, and we know. This can be deeply liberating. We are not bound by the judgments of others because we understand our own hearts, past actions, and motives. If we maintain daily prayer and conversation with God, He walks beside us every step of the journey.

Ways to Build Trust Based on Christian Principles

- **Walk in Integrity (Proverbs 10:9)**
  Be the same person in private as you are in public. Integrity creates predictability, and predictability builds trust.
- **Keep Your Word (Matthew 5:37)**
  Let your "yes" be yes and your "no" be no. Following through, even on small things, builds credibility over time.
- **Speak the Truth in Love (Ephesians 4:15)**
  Honesty builds trust, but gentle honesty preserves relationships. Truth without love wounds. Love without truth misleads.
- **Own Your Mistakes (1 John 1:9)**
  Admit when you fall short. Confession is not weakness. It demonstrates humility and maturity.
- **Forgive Freely (Colossians 3:13)**
  Trust deepens when people know they are safe even when imperfect. Forgiveness keeps relationships from eroding.
- **Serve Others Selflessly (Mark 10:45)**
  Service builds trust because it shows your intentions come from love, not self-gain.
- **Be Slow to Speak and Quick to Listen (James 1:19)**
  Listening communicates value. Being understood creates a foundation for trust.

- **Practice Consistency (Galatians 6:9)**
  People trust what they can count on. Consistent actions, character, and compassion create security.
- **Guard Confidentiality (Proverbs 11:13)**
  Keep confidences. Nothing erodes trust faster than sharing what was meant to be private.
- **Show Grace, Not Judgment (John 1:14)**
  Jesus came full of grace and truth. Leaders who extend grace create environments where people feel safe to be honest.
- **Seek God's Wisdom Daily (James 1:5)**
  Trustworthiness grows when decisions flow from prayer, Scripture, and spiritual discernment.
- **Love Sacrificially (John 13:34–35)**
  Jesus said love is the mark of His disciples. Love that costs us something is the most powerful trust-builder of all.

A Moment When I Lost Trust

While the list above highlights many ways to build trust, it can also be lost quickly. Reflecting on my leadership journey, one moment stands out clearly. Even now, I wish I had handled it differently.

It involved a conversation with a nursing leader who was overwhelmed by workload and responsibilities. She had come to me with concerns before, and I offered what guidance I could. I also asked her to return if those concerns continued. Time passed, and I assumed things had improved.

Then one day she came to my office at a breaking point. She was exhausted, discouraged, and her frustration felt directed at me. My first reaction was frustration that she hadn't returned sooner, as I had requested. And to be candid, I was carrying the weight of my own stress and pressure at the time. I wasn't as compassionate as I should have been.

I felt that some of the responsibilities she struggled with were simply part of the expectations of her role. My response to her was honest, but it was not as gentle or loving as it should have been. The relationship never recovered, and she soon left the organization.

How Trust Is Lost

Trust can erode quietly, often through small conversations and subtle interactions. It may be our words, tone, or even our body language. It can come from a lack of warmth, support, or understanding. Failing to extend grace is often enough to undermine trust over time. Common ways leaders lose trust include:

- **Inconsistency between words and actions**
  Saying one thing but doing another, even in small ways, quickly erodes credibility.
- **Reacting emotionally instead of responding thoughtfully**
  Sharp words, harsh tones, or visible frustration can overshadow your message.
- **Minimizing someone's concerns**
  Telling people "it's part of the job" or "you'll be fine" when they are struggling makes them feel unseen.
- **Failing to follow through**
  Missed promises, deadlines, or check-ins chip away at trust.
- **Being unavailable or unapproachable**
  A leader who is consistently too busy, distracted, or closed off communicates that people do not matter.
- **Showing favoritism or uneven treatment**
  Inconsistent standards or perceived inequality undermine trust.
- **Avoiding hard conversations**
  Sidestepping issues that need addressing erodes confidence in your courage and fairness.
- **Speaking negatively about others**
  Criticizing someone behind their back creates suspicion that you might do the same to them.
- **Withholding information**
  Guarding what people need to know breeds insecurity and mistrust.
- **Not admitting mistakes**
  Shifting blame or pretending everything is fine destroys authenticity and respect.
- **Taking credit but not giving it**
  Failing to recognize others' contributions makes leaders seem self-centered and insecure.

- **Correcting publicly while praising privately**
  Public embarrassment leaves lasting wounds, while public affirmation builds trust.

How to Build Trust Consistently

Building trust consistently begins with reflecting on our past actions and current relationships. As you read the lists of ways to build and lose trust, you may recall moments you wish you could change. That is part of being human. What matters most is treating each day as a gift and a fresh opportunity to start anew.

For some, this means continuing to strengthen high-trust relationships that have grown over time. For others, it may mean repairing connections where trust has weakened. Restoring trust is not easy, but it is possible through authenticity, honesty, and humility. Sometimes it also means beginning new relationships with a renewed commitment to high-trust behaviors from the very start.

Consistency comes from choosing these behaviors each day. It is not a one-time effort but a way of life. It means showing up with integrity, listening with intention, and extending grace freely. It also means trusting God and, over time, building a track record that helps you trust yourself.

Every day offers a chance to realign your heart and renew your commitment. You will not do this perfectly, but consistency over time shapes a life defined by character and trustworthiness. When you place your trust in God, He will equip you to become a person others can depend on, and your life will reflect that trust to everyone around you.

Action Step 1: Reflect Daily

Take a few minutes each day to honestly examine your words, actions, and motives. Ask God to reveal where you can grow and strengthen your integrity.

Action Step 2: Practice Christlike Behaviors

Intentionally walk in integrity, speak truth in love, extend grace, and serve others selflessly. Consistency in these small actions compounds into trust over time.

Action Step 3: Repair and Strengthen Relationships

Reach out to those with whom trust has been strained. Listen actively, own mistakes, and show humility and care.

Action Step 4: Live with Transparency and Accountability

Keep your commitments, guard confidences, and stay accountable to God and trusted mentors. Let your yes be yes and your no be no so others know they can rely on you.

Reflection and Journal Prompts

1. When have you struggled to trust yourself in the past, and what did you learn from that experience? How can you strengthen your integrity moving forward?
2. In what areas of your relationships or decisions do you need to rely more fully on God's wisdom? How can daily prayer and reflection help you act with integrity?
3. Think of a recent interaction where trust was either strengthened or weakened. What behaviors contributed to that outcome, and what could you do differently next time?
4. Who in your life would benefit if you intentionally extended more grace, honesty, or reliability? How can you create a ripple of trust in your relationships this week?

Lesson 24

Reflect Christ in Conflict

Conflict is inevitable in leadership, but how we respond reveals who we are and whom we follow. Reflecting Christ in moments of tension means choosing patience over defensiveness, humility over pride, and reconciliation over winning. When we allow the Holy Spirit to guide our words, we bring peace into situations that might otherwise escalate. By anchoring ourselves in Christlike character, we not only resolve conflict more effectively but also model a different way of leading marked by grace, truth, and a steady, faith-filled presence.

At times, this is easier said than done, but it is essential. If people remember nothing else, they will remember how we respond to conflict. It shapes their trust in us and how they perceive our character. One mishandled exchange can create an impression that is difficult to undo, and word spreads quickly. Reacting with anger, frustration, or bitterness leaves a scar, including the tone we use and the words we choose.

Tools for Reflecting Christ in Conflict

Because our response to conflict carries a lasting impact, it is important to approach these moments with intention rather than impulse. The tools below provide practical guidance for reflecting Christ in the midst of difficult conversations.

DOI: 10.4324/9781003769781-27

- **Pause before responding.** A short moment of silence allows emotions to settle and gives you space to respond with clarity instead of reacting out of frustration.
- **Ask clarifying questions.** Many conflicts escalate because of assumptions. A simple question such as, "Help me understand what you meant" can prevent unnecessary tension.
- **Focus on the issue, not the person.** Address the behavior, misunderstanding, or problem rather than making judgments about someone's character.
- **Seek understanding before being understood.** Listening fully communicates respect and opens the door for a more productive and Christlike conversation.
- **Pray for wisdom.** Even a brief inward prayer can re-center your heart and help you lead with humility and peace.

The Power of Mental Reframing

The power of mental reframing cannot be overstated, especially when emotions begin to rise. Anger, frustration, anxiety, and fear can feel powerful and overwhelming. In these moments, it is easy to forget our commitment to reflect a Christlike presence. Yet God gives us strength when we ask Him, and reframing a situation can make it far more likely that we will respond with wisdom rather than react out of emotion.

Let me offer a personal example related to my children. I have two beautiful daughters whom I love very much, and it is important to me to remain calm, centered, and patient. But anyone who has children knows how challenging that can be. There was a season when one of my daughters was young and frequently struggled with anger and tantrums. It often felt as though nothing I said or did made a difference, and at times it seemed almost impossible not to be drawn into the emotion of the moment.

Two ideas from parenting books helped me reframe that season. The first was the image of a rollercoaster and the reminder that I did not have to get on the emotional ride with my child. I could remain grounded and create space between myself and the swirling emotion around me. The second idea was even more powerful and ultimately changed how I responded. It reminded me that while the season would pass, how my daughter remembered my reactions would stay with her. That realization shifted everything.

Reframing works the same way in leadership. There are often multiple ways to view a situation, and healthier perspectives frequently benefit both us and those we lead. As leaders, we can ask ourselves the same question I asked as a parent: How do I want to be remembered? God brings people into our lives for many reasons, including our own growth, and few remain with us for our entire journey. When a season with a team or an organization comes to an end, how do we want them to look back on our presence? Ultimately, our reactions in moments of conflict become an important part of the legacy we leave behind.

Letting Go of Being Right

For many of us, conflict is difficult because we feel we are right. That may be true, but in many cases it doesn't matter. How you respond will immediately affect your relationship with the other person and may be difficult to recover from. In addition, word often spreads quickly. This is far more important than whether you were correct about a particular issue.

Consider how these situations typically unfold. It can be hard to control emotions in moments of conflict. The other person may act with arrogance, pride, or bitterness. Their words or tone may be condescending or demeaning. Does that matter? Not really. If anything, it is further reason to let it go.

Remember that it takes two people to escalate a conflict. Often, the best strategy is to disengage immediately. This goes against human nature, but it becomes easier when we ask for God's help. Never underestimate the power of intention. With genuine desire and continued effort, change is possible. Even if mistakes occur, consistent commitment builds healthier habits over time. Guidance from Scripture reinforces this approach:

> If it is possible, as far as it depends on you, live at peace with everyone.
>
> Romans 12:18 (NIV)

Responding this way requires patience, humility, and determination. But every time you choose a Christlike response, it is a success worth celebrating. You can take healthy satisfaction in your self-control, knowing that God is pleased. Over time, this approach strengthens relationships not only with the individual involved but also with others who observe your conduct. Gradually, you will become known as a steady presence, someone who responds with grace, is not easily rattled, and can be trusted with greater responsibility.

That said, there are times when you cannot simply let things go. If someone on your team behaves abusively toward you or others, the situation must be addressed promptly, privately, and respectfully. Behavior that crosses a clear line can harm both the team and the organization's culture. Likewise, executive decisions sometimes require firm action. In those cases, you can thank others for their input while clearly explaining your perspective and the reasons for your decision.

In the end, reflecting Christ in conflict is not about perfection but about direction. It is about repeatedly choosing to align your reactions with Christ's character rather than with your impulses. You will not always get it right, but every step toward patience, humility, kindness, and self-control strengthens your witness and shapes your legacy. God honors every sincere effort to seek His help, pause before speaking, and see others through His eyes. As you continue to practice these habits, you will become the kind of leader who brings peace into tense situations, lifts others instead of escalating conflict, and leaves a lasting impression of grace wherever you go.

Action Step 1: Pause and Pray Before Responding

Take a brief moment to breathe, center yourself, and ask God for guidance. Use the question, "But is it kind?" to frame your response and prevent reactive emotions from driving your words or tone.

Action Step 2: Reframe the Situation

When emotions rise, intentionally consider a perspective that promotes understanding and peace. Ask yourself how your response will impact relationships, your witness as a leader, and how you want to be remembered.

Action Step 3: Focus on the Issue, Not the Person

Address the behavior, misunderstanding, or problem rather than judging or labeling the individual. Separate the person from the actions so that your response reflects Christlike humility and respect.

Action Step 4: Disengage When Necessary and Respond with Grace

Recognize when a conflict crosses a line or when an executive decision must be made. Handle these situations privately, respectfully, and professionally, clearly communicating your perspective while maintaining a spirit of peace and integrity.

Journal and Reflection Prompts

1. Think of a recent conflict you experienced. How did you respond in the moment? Were your words, tone, and actions aligned with Christlike character? What would you do differently if you could respond again?
2. Are there recurring triggers that make it difficult for you to respond with patience or humility? What emotions or situations tend to push you toward defensiveness or anger? How can you prepare in advance to respond differently?
3. Consider a current or recent challenging situation. How could you reframe it in a way that focuses on understanding, peace, and relationship rather than "being right" or winning? How might this change your response?
4. Reflect on how you want to be remembered by those you lead and interact with. How do your responses to conflict today contribute to that legacy? What steps can you take to ensure your actions consistently reflect grace, integrity, and Christlike character?

Lesson 25

Handle Criticism with Grace

All leaders face criticism, regardless of role, sector, or intention. In healthcare, it can be especially frequent. There are simply not enough resources to meet the expectations of all groups, including patients, families, nurses, physicians, surveyors, the media, and accreditation agencies.

Some criticism may be clearly unjustified. Other criticism may be understandable but directed at the wrong people. For example, it is often easier to blame local hospital leaders than to confront the complexity of the healthcare system itself. Some criticism may be fair, offering an opportunity for reflection and growth. Regardless, healthcare leaders encounter these judgments regularly.

Stepping into leadership in such an environment requires real courage. I know this from experience. As a healthcare CEO, I felt the weight of leadership every day, from the moment I accepted the role until the day I stepped away many years later.

With that in mind, you should be proud of yourself. It takes strength to step into these roles and even more to remain in them over time. Compassion and empathy, the very qualities that draw us to healthcare, can make criticism feel especially personal. Even so, some criticism can be valuable if received as feedback, and the best leaders use it to grow and improve. For Christian healthcare leaders, handling criticism with humility and grace is both a professional and spiritual calling. This calling is reflected in Scripture, and in the life and example of Christ Himself.

DOI: 10.4324/9781003769781-28

A Biblical Example of Handling Criticism with Grace

After His arrest in the garden, Jesus was taken to the home of the high priest, where the Sanhedrin, the ruling council, had gathered in the middle of the night. It was a rushed and irregular trial, driven more by fear and political pressure than by any search for truth. One witness after another offered accusations meant to condemn Him, yet their testimonies contradicted one another. Even when the leaders tried to shape a charge that would hold, the evidence remained weak. Through it all, Jesus stood quietly, refusing to defend Himself against the falsehoods being spoken.

Finally, the high priest demanded that Jesus declare whether He was the Messiah. Breaking His silence, Jesus spoke the truth, fully aware that this confession would seal the council's verdict. The leaders responded with outrage, tearing their robes, mocking Him, and striking Him. He absorbed their hostility without retaliation, entrusting Himself entirely to His Father's justice.

Because the Sanhedrin lacked authority to execute Him, they delivered Jesus to Pontius Pilate, the Roman governor. Before Pilate, the charges shifted. No longer accused of blasphemy, He was now portrayed as a political threat, one who opposed Roman rule and claimed kingship. Pilate questioned Him, asking whether He was truly the King of the Jews. Jesus answered briefly and calmly, offering no attempt to plead His case or protest the twisting of His words.

As the religious leaders hurled accusation after accusation, Jesus remained silent, and His composure astonished Pilate. The governor could see that Jesus had been handed over out of envy, not guilt. Pilate attempted several times to release Him, appealing to a Passover custom, sending Him to Herod, and heeding a warning from his wife. The crowd, stirred by the leaders, shouted all the louder for crucifixion. Pilate eventually yielded, washing his hands to claim innocence even as he authorized the execution.

Jesus accepted the sentence without bitterness, anger, or struggle. He spoke the truth where it mattered and remained silent where nothing He said would change hardened hearts. Even in the face of false accusations, manipulation, and injustice, His dignity never wavered. He trusted His Father completely, showing courage and grace that remain unmatched. His example is a model for anyone who has ever been misunderstood, misjudged, or unfairly criticized.

Parallels for Healthcare Leaders

As an organizational leader, there are lessons to be drawn from this story. The stakes may not be as high, but they can feel intense in the moment. You may fear losing your position, your influence, or control. You may be falsely accused or misrepresented. Your reputation may be questioned when public criticism focuses on your integrity, intentions, or motivations. In those moments, responding with humility and grace can feel difficult. The most natural response is often self-protection, but reacting impulsively rather than reflecting can be a mistake. Remember the words of Peter:

> When they hurled their insults at him, he did not retaliate; when he suffered, he made no threats. Instead, he entrusted himself to him who judges justly.
>
> 1 Peter 2:23 (NIV)

You can trust God as well. He knows your thoughts, actions, and intentions. Ground your leadership in your relationship with Him. Then speak honestly, with humility and grace, when criticism occurs. Remain calm, centered, and transparent. Remember that criticism is often rooted in hurt or fear. This can be hard to see when all you notice is anger and bitterness, but those emotions are commonly present just beneath the surface.

How to Handle Criticism with Grace

There are concrete tools you can use to make handling criticism easier. You always have a choice in how you frame a situation and can decide in advance how you will respond.

- **Pause and Reflect**
  Take a moment before responding. Breathe, collect your thoughts, and resist the urge to react immediately.
- **Separate Emotion from Feedback**
  Acknowledge your feelings, but focus on the content of the criticism rather than personal attacks.
- **Seek Understanding**
  Ask clarifying questions if needed. Understanding the perspective behind the criticism helps you respond thoughtfully.

- **Look for the Lesson**
  Even in unfair criticism, there may be an element of truth or an opportunity to grow.
- **Respond with Humility**
  Use calm, respectful language. Avoid defensiveness, sarcasm, or blame.
- **Decide What to Act On**
  Not all criticism requires action. Discern what is useful and what can be set aside.
- **Forgive and Let Go**
  Release lingering resentment or hurt. Holding onto anger only weighs you down and can cloud future interactions.
- **Maintain Perspective**
  Remember your values and mission. Criticism does not define your worth or your leadership.

The Power of Intention

The power of intention cannot be overstated. It takes real strength to overcome the natural instinct toward self-protection and defensiveness. But as followers of Christ, we have the ultimate example before us. Every moment in which you choose to respond to criticism with humility and grace is a moment worth celebrating. As a healthcare leader, you will have many opportunities to practice this discipline.

Real change begins in these small moments. When you respond with grace, peace, and forgiveness, you create the possibility of transformation in others. Maybe not immediately, but sometimes much later. Undeserved grace is powerful. It stays with people and opens doors that defensiveness never will.

You also model something profound for the leaders and staff around you. Word spreads quickly in any organization. Whether you respond with calm or hostility, others will take note and often follow your example. Over time, this shapes the culture, weaving grace and emotional safety into the fabric of the workplace. In healthcare, this creates a spiritually and mentally healthy environment for healing, not only for patients but for staff as well.

Responding to criticism with grace does more than preserve your own character. You are helping to heal someone who may be hurting far more than you realize. You are choosing the way of Jesus, one intentional moment at a time.

Action Step 1: Pause and Pray

Before responding to criticism, take a deep breath and pray for wisdom, patience, and clarity. Ask God to help you see the situation from His perspective and respond with humility.

Action Step 2: Listen Actively

Focus on understanding the other person's perspective. Ask questions if needed and resist the urge to interrupt or defend yourself. Sometimes being heard is more important than being right.

Action Step 3: Respond Thoughtfully, Not Emotionally

Choose words that reflect respect and grace. Speak truth gently, avoid defensiveness, and stay aligned with your values and mission.

Action Step 4: Reflect and Learn

After the interaction, review what happened. Identify any lessons, areas for personal growth, or patterns you can address proactively. Then, forgive and release any lingering resentment.

Reflection and Journal Prompts

1. Think about a recent time you received criticism, whether fair or unfair. How did you respond? What emotions came up, and how might you handle a similar situation differently with grace?
2. Reflect on criticism you've received that had some amount of truth. What lessons or insights can you take from it to improve your leadership or character?

3. When facing criticism, what is your natural instinct: to defend, to explain, or to react emotionally? How can you align your response more intentionally with humility and Christlike grace?
4. Imagine responding to criticism calmly, thoughtfully, and with empathy. How does this change the outcome for you, the critic, and your team? What steps can you take to make this your default approach?

Lesson 26

Speak Hard Truths with a Soft Heart

One of the most difficult aspects of leadership is engaging in hard conversations. These moments often require sharing information that is uncomfortable or unwelcome. The goal is to communicate truthfully while preserving trust, respect, and dignity. However, despite our best intentions, others may still respond defensively or feel misunderstood.

In response, some leaders instinctively harden themselves as a form of self-protection. They may become overly firm, emotionally distant, or rush through the conversation to get it over with. While understandable, this posture does not reflect a Christlike presence.

A compassionate approach keeps the door open for deeper and more honest dialogue. This may occur later, after time for reflection. By contrast, a cold or rigid approach can close that door immediately. In a single moment, trust may be damaged, vulnerability may feel unsafe, and a relationship may struggle to recover.

Guidance from Scripture

As Christian leaders, it is helpful to reflect on guidance from Scripture:

> Instead, speaking the truth in love, we will grow to become in every respect the mature body of him who is the head, that is, Christ.
>
> Ephesians 4:15 (NIV)

DOI: 10.4324/9781003769781-29

Ephesians 4 emphasizes unity and maturity within the body of Christ, the Church. Paul encourages believers to live in ways that strengthen the community and reflect Christ's character. Spiritual maturity, he reminds us, is not merely personal. It develops within community. We grow best when we are honest with one another in ways that are loving and constructive. This balance of truth and love also provides guidance for healthcare organizations. When leaders communicate honestly with compassion, teams are strengthened, trust is reinforced, and the organization becomes more effective in fulfilling its mission.

Practical Strategies for Gentle Truth Telling

Speaking hard truths with a soft heart does not happen by accident. It requires intentionality and preparation. Leaders can use several strategies to communicate honestly while preserving trust, respect, and dignity.

- **Prepare Thoughtfully**
  Before entering a difficult conversation, take time to clarify its purpose and desired outcome. Consider the facts carefully and anticipate possible reactions. Preparation helps ensure that the conversation remains focused on the issue rather than being driven by emotion or misunderstanding.
- **Begin with Affirmation**
  Starting with acknowledgment of the individual's strengths or contributions sets a positive tone. Recognizing what someone does well does not diminish the truth that must be addressed. Instead, it demonstrates respect and helps the person feel valued. For example, a leader might say, "I appreciate the effort you put into managing the patient schedule. I would like to discuss an area where we can improve even further."
- **Use "I" Statements**
  Framing feedback from your own perspective can reduce defensiveness. Phrases such as "I noticed" or "I am concerned about" focus on your observations and concerns rather than placing blame. This approach aligns with speaking the truth in love because it communicates honesty without accusation.

- **Invite Dialogue**
  Rather than delivering a verdict, invite the other person to share their perspective. Open-ended questions such as, "Can you help me understand what happened here?" or "How do you see this situation?" foster mutual understanding and reinforce that the conversation is a dialogue, not a one-sided critique.
- **Pause and Allow Reflection**
  After sharing feedback, allow space for the individual to process what has been said. Silence can feel uncomfortable, but it provides time for reflection and signals patience and respect. Immediate responses are not always constructive, and thoughtful pauses can help prevent defensiveness from escalating.

By incorporating these strategies, leaders can create an environment in which difficult conversations become opportunities for growth rather than moments of tension.

The Role of Listening

Speaking truth in love is only one part of a successful conversation. Listening is equally important. When leaders listen actively, they demonstrate respect, empathy, and a genuine desire to understand. This posture can reduce defensiveness and strengthen trust.

- **Practice Active Listening**
  Active listening involves giving full attention to the speaker without interrupting or mentally preparing a response while the other person is speaking. Simple behaviors such as nodding, maintaining appropriate eye contact, and reflecting back what you hear, such as "So what I hear you saying is," communicate that the other person's perspective is valued.
- **Ask Clarifying Questions**
  Encourage dialogue by asking open-ended questions that invite the individual to explain their thoughts and feelings. Questions such as "Can you walk me through how you approached this situation?" or "What challenges did you encounter?" foster understanding and convey curiosity rather than judgment.
- **Avoid Immediate Judgment**
  Even when mistakes are clear, resist the urge to respond immediately with correction or criticism. Taking time to listen first allows the

individual to express themselves fully and signals that the conversation is a collaborative effort rather than a lecture.

- **Show Empathy**
  Listening with empathy means acknowledging emotions and challenges without excusing errors. Statements such as "I understand this was a difficult situation for you" validate feelings while maintaining a focus on learning and improvement.
- **Encourage Reflection**
  At times, listening itself creates space for the individual to recognize areas for change. By allowing time for reflection, leaders foster conversations that are constructive and transformational rather than defensive or punitive.

Handling Defensive or Emotional Responses

Even when truth is spoken with care, individuals may still respond defensively, emotionally, or with confusion. Leaders who anticipate these reactions are better equipped to respond in ways that preserve trust and encourage growth.

- **Expect Emotional Reactions**
  It is natural for individuals to feel hurt, embarrassed, or frustrated when receiving difficult feedback. Recognizing this ahead of time helps leaders remain calm and empathetic, rather than becoming defensive themselves.
- **Respond with Empathy**
  When someone reacts emotionally, acknowledge their feelings without compromising the truth. Statements such as "I understand this is difficult to hear" or "I can see why you might feel that way" communicate care while keeping the conversation constructive.
- **Maintain Composure**
  A leader's calm presence can prevent escalation. Even when emotions run high, staying composed models emotional maturity and helps create a safer environment for honest dialogue.
- **Reframe the Conversation if Needed**
  If a discussion becomes too heated, it may be appropriate to pause or redirect the focus. For example, a leader might say, "Let's take a moment and revisit this in a few minutes so we can both reflect".

This reinforces that the goal is growth and understanding rather than winning an argument.

- **Reaffirm the Relationship**
  Conclude the conversation by affirming the relationship and expressing mutual respect. Remind the individual of shared goals and your commitment to their development. This step strengthens trust and supports long-term collaboration.

By anticipating emotional responses and responding with empathy and composure, leaders can transform tense moments into opportunities for understanding and growth. This reflects the balance of truth and love described in Ephesians 4:15 and fosters maturity within individuals and across the team.

The Long-Term Value of Trust

As I reflect on my leadership journey, there have been moments when I handled difficult conversations well and others when I fell short. Like most leaders, I have grown over time by learning which approaches foster trust, understanding, and growth. If you recognize similar experiences in your own journey, extend grace to yourself for past mistakes.

What matters most is not perfection, but commitment. Renewing your dedication to speak truth in love, to listen actively, and to lead with empathy strengthens leadership over time. When these practices are applied consistently, relationships deepen, trust grows, and teams are better equipped to thrive together. Just as Ephesians 4:15 reminds us, maturity and unity develop when truth and love guide our words and actions, both in our personal lives and in the communities we lead.

Action Step 1: Prepare Before Difficult Conversations

Take time to clarify the purpose, gather facts, and anticipate possible reactions. Consider how to frame your feedback in a way that preserves trust and demonstrates respect.

Action Step 2: Speak Truth in Love

Use "I" statements, begin with affirmation, and invite dialogue. Focus on honesty without blame, keeping your tone gentle and your words constructive.

Action Step 3: Listen Actively and Empathetically

Practice active listening, ask clarifying questions, and acknowledge emotions. Allow the individual space to reflect and process, ensuring the conversation is collaborative rather than one-sided.

Action Step 4: Build Long-Term Trust

Respond to emotional reactions with composure and empathy. Reaffirm relationships, forgive past mistakes, and commit to consistently practicing these principles to strengthen both personal and team growth.

Reflection and Journal Prompts

1. Reflect on a time when you had to deliver difficult feedback. How did you approach it? Did your words and tone preserve trust and dignity, or could they have been more compassionate? What would you do differently now?
2. Consider your current leadership practices. How well do you balance honesty with empathy in your interactions? Are there specific situations where you tend to lean more toward bluntness or avoidance?
3. Think about a recent conversation where someone reacted defensively or emotionally. How well did you listen and acknowledge their perspective? How could active listening and empathy have improved the outcome?
4. Identify one specific way you can renew your commitment to speaking truth in love this week. How will you apply this principle to strengthen trust, build relationships, and promote growth in your team or organization?

Lesson 27

Forgive Freely

Leadership in healthcare is demanding. Mistakes will happen, people will disappoint you, and the system may often feel as though it is working against you. In moments like these, forgiveness is more than a spiritual ideal. It becomes a vital practice for sustaining your heart, mind, and effectiveness as a leader.

This includes forgiving those who helped shape the system, forgiving those who criticize you, and perhaps most difficult of all, forgiving yourself. Leadership carries the weight of expectation and the pressure to respond without faltering. But wise leaders recognize that healthcare is a collaborative effort and many challenges have no simple or immediate solutions.

Forgiveness vs. Acceptance of Abuse

At the same time, it is essential to distinguish forgiveness from tolerating harm. Forgiveness means releasing anger, resentment, and the desire for revenge. It does not mean condoning harmful behavior, excusing injustice, or pretending harm never occurred.

Forgiveness is about reclaiming your peace, protecting your well-being, and making space for healing and growth. It does not require you to accept ongoing verbal, emotional, or physical abuse. Healthcare workers operate in high-risk environments, and every person deserves safety, respect, and dignity. Healthy leadership requires clear boundaries and a zero-tolerance stance toward abusive behavior.

 DOI: 10.4324/9781003769781-30

The Biblical Foundation for Forgiveness

Scripture presents forgiveness not merely as a moral ideal but as a path to spiritual wholeness. It is both a divine calling and a practical discipline that shapes how we lead, respond to conflict, and cultivate resilience. Forgiveness flows from the grace we ourselves have received and is essential to the health of our relationships. Withholding forgiveness burdens the heart, while releasing it brings spiritual and emotional freedom. The New Testament consistently frames forgiveness as a response to God's grace and a defining mark of Christian maturity:

> Bear with each other and forgive one another if any of you has a grievance against someone. Forgive as the Lord forgave you.
>
> Colossians 3:13 (NIV)

Jesus reinforces that forgiveness is not optional or occasional, but a continual posture of the heart, especially in relationships marked by repeated offense:

> Then Peter came to Jesus and asked, 'Lord, how many times shall I forgive my brother or sister who sins against me? Up to seven times?' Jesus answered, 'I tell you, not seven times, but seventy-seven times.'
>
> Matthew 18:21–22 (NIV)

Forgiveness also involves releasing our desire for vengeance and entrusting justice to God rather than allowing resentment to take root. This is especially significant for leaders who experience criticism, conflict, or perceived unfairness:

> Do not repay anyone evil for evil. Be careful to do what is right in the eyes of everyone. If it is possible, as far as it depends on you, live at peace with everyone. Do not take revenge, my dear friends, but leave room for God's wrath, for it is written: 'It is mine to avenge; I will repay,' says the Lord.
>
> Romans 12:17–19 (NIV)

Even in the face of profound injustice, Jesus models forgiveness as a source of peace and reconciliation:

> Jesus said, 'Father, forgive them, for they do not know what they are doing.'
>
> Luke 23:34 (NIV)

Taken together, these passages show that forgiveness is not a denial of wrongdoing, nor is it a sign of weakness. It is a deliberate act of trust in God that frees the heart, strengthens relationships, and sustains leaders over the long term. For those called to lead in complex and demanding environments, forgiveness becomes an essential practice for both spiritual formation and effective leadership.

Applying Forgiveness in Healthcare Leadership

Having explored the scriptural foundation for forgiveness, we can now consider how it shapes daily leadership practice:

- **Acknowledge Your Feelings**
  Recognize and honor feelings such as anger, sadness, or frustration. Journaling or speaking with a trusted mentor can help process these emotions constructively.
- **Separate the Person from the Behavior**
  Focus on the specific actions or words that caused harm rather than assigning judgment to the person's character.
- **Set Healthy Boundaries**
  Forgiveness does not grant permission for continued harm. Clearly define unacceptable behaviors and take appropriate steps to protect yourself and your team.
- **Release Resentment and Let Go of Grudges**
  Forgiveness is often a process rather than a single decision. Consciously choose to release resentment and the desire for revenge over time.
- **Practice Self-Forgiveness**
  Leadership requires humility, learning, and growth. Release guilt that hinders reflection, renewal, and forward movement.
- **Reflect on God's Forgiveness**
  Return to Scripture for perspective and strength. Allow God's grace to remind you how deeply you are forgiven.

- **Model Forgiveness for Others**
  A leader's posture shapes organizational culture. Modeling forgiveness fosters trust, psychological safety, and compassionate accountability.
- **Seek Reconciliation Where Possible**
  When it is safe and mutually desired, work toward restoring relationships. Reconciliation should never be forced.

A Reflection on the Difficulty of Forgiveness

Even with biblical guidance, forgiveness can be deeply challenging. Forgiving someone does not erase the emotional impact of their actions. You may still feel hurt, anxious, or guarded around them. You may genuinely desire to forgive yet struggle with lingering anger or disappointment.

These emotions are real and deserve acknowledgment. Forgiveness is a decision to release resentment, not the immediate elimination of emotional pain. Healing takes time, and lingering feelings do not mean your forgiveness is insincere. They simply reflect your humanity.

The key question then becomes this: What will you do with the emotions that remain after forgiveness? Recognizing them, rather than suppressing them, is the first step toward true healing. The following practices can help you process and release what remains.

Techniques to Release Lingering Emotions

- **Meditation and Guided Visualizations (10–20 minutes)**
  Sit comfortably, close your eyes, and slow your breathing. Spend a few minutes relaxing your body from head to toe, allowing each exhale to release tension and emotional weight. Continue breathing steadily as you visualize a warm, calming light moving through your body, softening tightness and easing stress. Remain in this relaxed state for 10–20 minutes. Many mindfulness apps offer guided meditations and visualizations designed to calm the nervous system, release stored emotions, and foster a grounded state.
- **Journaling**
  Write about your feelings in a structured way to clarify thoughts and emotions. Reflect on what forgiveness might look like in this situation and what steps are within your control.

- **Prayer or Spiritual Reflection**
  Use prayer to seek guidance, perspective, and strength. Meditate on passages related to forgiveness, grace, and renewal.
- **Physical Release Techniques**
  Gentle movement, stretching, or exercise can help release stored tension and emotional energy. Even a short walk can provide mental clarity and emotional distance.
- **Breathing Exercises**
  Deep, intentional breathing helps reduce the body's stress response to anger or anxiety. Techniques such as box breathing (inhale, hold, exhale, hold for equal counts) are simple and effective.
- **Cognitive Reframing**
  Re-examine the situation from a broader perspective, considering context, human imperfection, or lessons learned. This approach reduces emotional reactivity and supports intentional, sustainable forgiveness.

Closing Reflection

Forgiveness is not a single act but a continual practice. It frees the heart, protects peace, and allows leaders to act with clarity and compassion. Even when emotions linger, acknowledging them and using practical tools such as meditation, journaling, prayer, and healthy boundaries helps you move forward with integrity.

Forgiveness is also an act of leadership. By extending grace to others and to yourself, you foster a culture where people can heal, grow, and bring their best to the vital work of caring for others. Leaders who forgive freely build environments marked by trust, resilience, and compassion. In doing so, they reflect the heart of God to the teams they serve.

Action Step 1: Identify One Person to Forgive This Week

Reflect on someone you have been holding resentment toward. Take a small step toward forgiveness, whether it's a mental release, prayer, or a compassionate conversation.

Action Step 2: Practice Daily Reflection and Mindfulness Techniques

Spend 5–10 minutes each day noticing lingering feelings of anger, hurt, or frustration. Use mindfulness, journaling, or guided visualization to release these emotions and maintain emotional clarity.

Action Step 3: Set or Reinforce Healthy Boundaries

Evaluate areas where toxic behavior exists in your personal or work environment. Clearly define what is acceptable and take steps to protect yourself and your team, while maintaining a forgiving heart.

Action Step 4: Model Forgiveness Publicly

Demonstrate grace in your interactions, acknowledge mistakes, guide others with patience, and offer constructive feedback. Show your team that forgiveness is both a personal practice and a leadership value, shaping the culture around you.

Reflection and Journal Prompts

1. Who do I find difficult to forgive, and why? What emotions come up when I think about this person or situation?
2. What decisions or actions have I struggled to forgive myself for? How might extending grace to myself change my perspective or leadership approach?
3. Are there situations where I need to forgive while still maintaining healthy boundaries? How can I release resentment without compromising my safety or team well-being?
4. What actions have I taken this week toward forgiveness, either for others or myself? What was challenging, and what did I learn about the impact of forgiveness on my leadership and personal peace?

Lesson 28

Be Authentic

You may have heard that authenticity is essential for effective leadership, but what does it really mean? At its core, authenticity is about being true to who you are and being at peace with how God has created you. Authentic leaders lead from this place of clarity, regardless of circumstances. For Christian healthcare leaders, authenticity is rooted not in self-expression alone, but in the indwelling presence of Jesus Christ, shaping how we lead, interact, and make decisions.

At the same time, authenticity is not a license to be careless, disrespectful, or dismissive of boundaries. When aspects of our character begin to hinder our leadership or negatively affect how others experience us, it signals an opportunity for reflection and growth. By holding authenticity and professionalism together, we model Christ-centered leadership that inspires trust, nurtures healthy relationships, and strengthens our organizations.

Seeing the Through Line of Your Life

In my own journey, it took time, growth, and intentional self-reflection to understand who I truly was. While this clarity sometimes comes with age, it is not automatic. It requires effort, honesty, and a willingness to examine your inner life. Through ongoing prayer and honest conversations with God, this understanding can gradually emerge.

Who are you really? Who has God designed you to be? What are you called to do, and how does that calling align with the strengths you have

DOI: 10.4324/9781003769781-31

been given? We may catch glimpses of these truths throughout our lives, but they are often overshadowed by the expectations of others, the roles we feel pressured to fill, the fear of disappointing people, or the constant noise and busyness of daily life. Over time, these layers can bury our true selves until we hardly recognize who God created us to be. When we rediscover that identity, it often brings a profound sense of relief and freedom.

As I look back, I can see threads that were present long before I understood their significance. I was consistently drawn to work that involved caring for others, listening deeply, helping people heal, and creating space for growth. Whether in mental health, teaching, or nonprofit service, I found myself returning again and again to roles centered on compassion, guidance, and restoration.

Over time, I also discovered a passion for leadership. I was drawn not only to supporting individuals, but to strengthening the systems and organizations that shaped their lives. Organizational transformation, values-based decision-making, and helping teams rediscover purpose became natural extensions of the same calling I had carried from the beginning. What started as a desire to care for people grew into a desire to help create healthier environments, places where values mattered, dignity was honored, and mission was more than a slogan.

For many years, these interests felt disconnected, as though I were simply following opportunities as they appeared. It was only later, through prayer and reflection, that I began to see the pattern. These were not random roles or shifting passions, but consistent indicators of the person God was forming me to be. The common thread was a calling to walk with people in their struggles, nurture their strengths, and help both individuals and organizations move toward greater health and wholeness.

Recognizing this brought clarity and peace. It allowed me to see my path not as a series of unrelated steps, but as a purposeful journey guided by God's hand. This understanding now shapes how I lead, authentically, compassionately, and in alignment with the values God has placed on my heart.

Discovering Your Authentic Self

Every leader has a God-given identity, but it often takes time and intentional effort to uncover it. This process rarely follows a straight path, but it is one of the most important journeys you can take. The following practices can help you discover who God created you to be and how that identity can shape your leadership.

- **Pray and reflect in quiet**
  Ask God to reveal the strengths, gifts, and desires He has placed within you. Notice where you feel most alive, aligned, and at peace.
- **Reflect on recurring themes in your life**
  Look back over your experiences and identify patterns in what energizes you, what you care about deeply, and where you naturally contribute.
- **Notice what burdens your heart**
  The issues, needs, or people that stir your compassion can point toward your calling.
- **Seek input from trusted people**
  Invite mentors, colleagues, or close friends to share what they see as your strengths and blind spots.
- **Observe where you have been fruitful**
  Consider settings where your efforts have created growth, healing, or positive change. These often align with your gifts.
- **Examine what drains you**
  Activities or roles that repeatedly exhaust you may not fit who God designed you to be.
- **Align your identity with your values**
  Reflect on the principles that matter most and ensure your decisions, leadership style, and daily actions reflect them.
- **Stay open to growth and transformation**
  Your authentic self evolves over time as God refines your identity and calling.

Authenticity in Scripture

As you reflect on how to live and lead with authenticity, consider these passages from Scripture:

> For we are God's handiwork, created in Christ Jesus to do good works, which God prepared in advance for us to do.
>
> Ephesians 2:10 (NIV)

This verse highlights that authenticity begins with recognizing who God created you to be. Leadership rooted in Christ-centered authenticity flows from embracing your identity and pursuing the good works God has prepared for you.

> We have different gifts, according to the grace given to each of us.
> Romans 12:6 (NIV)

Here, Scripture reminds us that each person is uniquely equipped by God. Authentic leadership means embracing your distinct gifts, cultivating self-awareness, and confidently fulfilling your God-given role, without comparing yourself to others.

Leading with Authenticity

Once you truly understand who you are, it can bring a profound sense of relief. As the storms of life come and go, your inner self and your relationship with God remain steady. From this place of clarity, you can engage with others authentically, showing your true self in every interaction.

In today's volatile healthcare environment, this steady presence is desperately needed. It helps teams feel safe, grounded, and genuinely valued. At the same time, it enables you to guide others in discovering their own authentic selves, creating a ripple effect that strengthens the entire organization. Leading with authenticity is not only about personal integrity. It is a powerful way to cultivate trust, resilience, and purpose across the systems and people you serve, reflecting God's guidance in every decision and interaction.

Action Step 1: Engage in Regular Self-Reflection and Prayer

Set aside dedicated time to examine your strengths, gifts, values, and areas for growth. Ask God for clarity about who you are and the purpose He has for you.

Action Step 2: Identify Your Recurring Life Themes and Passions

Look back over your personal and professional experiences to notice patterns in what energizes you, where you have made an impact, and what truly matters to you.

Action Step 3: Seek Feedback from Trusted Mentors and Colleagues

Invite others to share their observations about your strengths, blind spots, and leadership style. Honest input helps you see yourself more clearly and grow in alignment with God's design.

Action Step 4: Lead Consistently from Your Authentic Self

Bring your values, gifts, and God-given identity into your daily leadership. Create environments where your team feels safe, valued, and inspired, and help others discover their own authentic selves.

Reflection and Journal Prompts

1. Reflect on your deepest values, strengths, and passions. How do these reflect the person God created you to be? In what ways are you currently expressing, or not expressing, your true self in your leadership and personal life?
2. Think about moments in your life and work when you felt energized, purposeful, or impactful. What patterns emerge? What do these experiences reveal about your God-given gifts and calling?
3. Identify external or internal pressures such as roles, cultural norms, or fear of disappointing others that may prevent you from fully living as your authentic self. How might God be inviting you to step beyond these barriers?
4. Consider your team, colleagues, or community. How can you create space for others to recognize and embrace their unique gifts and values? How can your authentic leadership inspire them to do so?

Lesson 29

Practice Servant Leadership

Servant leadership is a popular idea in leadership circles today, but its secular interpretation often misses its full meaning. At its heart, servant leadership is rooted in Scripture and modeled perfectly in the life of Christ. For Christian healthcare leaders, embracing this deeper, Christ-centered approach transforms not only how we lead, but how we serve and impact those around us.

What Sets Christian Servant Leadership Apart

Secular models often view servant leadership as a tool to build trust, improve morale, or boost organizational performance. Biblical servant leadership begins from a different place. It starts with the example of Jesus Christ, who serves not for strategic gain but out of love, humility, and obedience to God. This foundation shapes not only what Christian leaders do, but why and how they do it.

Christian servant leadership is less about perfect systems and more about embodying the heart of Christ within them. Your presence, humility, and willingness to serve become a stabilizing force, especially in challenging circumstances. Leaders who reflect Christ's character by listening well, valuing each person, and making decisions with compassion, create pockets of hope and trust. This is the kind of influence that endures, no matter the obstacles.

DOI: 10.4324/9781003769781-32

The Biblical Foundation of Servant Leadership

Scripture provides clear guidance on what servant leadership means for Christian leaders:

> Jesus called them together and said, 'You know that those who are regarded as rulers of the Gentiles lord it over them, and their high officials exercise authority over them. Not so with you. Instead, whoever wants to become great among you must be your servant, and whoever wants to be first must be slave of all. For even the Son of Man did not come to be served, but to serve, and to give his life as a ransom for many.'
>
> Mark 10:42–45 (NIV)

This passage offers a classic example of Christian servant leadership, emphasizing humility, service, and Christ's ultimate example of self-giving. Leadership, Jesus shows, is not about personal gain or authority. It is about serving others with love and integrity. This teaching is further illustrated in John 13:1–17, when Jesus washes his disciples' feet, a task considered lowly and menial. Here, servant leadership is modeled in action: humble, attentive, and willing to meet others' needs, even when the work is difficult or overlooked.

For Christian leaders, especially in healthcare, this demonstrates that leadership is not about status, recognition, or control, but about embodying the heart of Christ in every interaction. Just as Jesus met His disciples where they were, leaders can meet patients, colleagues, and staff with care, patience, and respect. By practicing servant-hearted leadership, Christian healthcare leaders foster trust, compassion, and hope, showing that true influence flows not from position or authority, but from a willingness to serve others faithfully.

Practical Applications in Healthcare

Christian healthcare leaders can embody servant leadership in practical ways:

- **Listen actively**
  Prioritize understanding staff and patients' needs and concerns before making decisions.

- **Demonstrate humility**
  Approach every role and task with a willingness to serve, regardless of status.
- **Serve behind the scenes**
  Take on tasks that may be overlooked or considered menial to support the team and model servant-hearted leadership.
- **Empower and mentor others**
  Help colleagues grow in skills, confidence, and professional development without seeking personal recognition.
- **Make compassionate, fair decisions**
  Consider how choices affect patients, families, and staff, emphasizing care over efficiency alone.
- **Cultivate trust and respect**
  Model ethical behavior, honesty, and integrity consistently.
- **Remain present in challenging moments**
  Offer encouragement, guidance, and support during high-stress or crisis situations.
- **Prioritize holistic well-being**
  Recognize the spiritual, emotional, and physical needs of patients and staff, not just their performance outcomes.

The Cost of Servant Leadership

Being a servant leader is not always easy. It often involves sacrifice, navigating conflict, and the risk of being misunderstood. One of the greatest challenges is balancing organizational pressures with spiritual integrity. It can be tempting to make decisions that protect your position or enhance your reputation. True servant leadership, however, requires courage to prioritize others, act with integrity, and follow Christ's example, even when it comes at a personal cost.

That said, leadership decisions are not always clear-cut. In my career, there were times when I had to reduce positions or cut expenses, knowing the real impact these decisions would have on those affected. Yet in tight financial situations, such actions may serve a greater good, allowing the organization to remain viable, continue its mission, and preserve the jobs of other employees.

How can you practice servant leadership in these difficult moments? Lead with transparency, empathy, and integrity. Communicate openly with those affected, acknowledge the impact on them, and offer support wherever possible. Maintain humility, admit the difficulty of the decision, and keep the organization's mission and the broader community in mind. Servant leadership is not about avoiding hard choices, but about how you make and carry them out, with care, courage, and a heart aligned with Christ. These are the real-world challenges leaders face today.

The Heart of Servant Leadership

Both secular and faith-based perspectives on servant leadership offer valuable insights. Each can strengthen the way we lead and serve. Yet when servant leadership is grounded in the example of Jesus, it gains a depth and power that reshapes both our character and our organizations.

When Jesus was asked about the greatest commandment, He taught that we are to love the Lord our God with all our heart, soul, and mind, and to love our neighbors as ourselves. Servant leadership is one of the most tangible ways to live out these commandments. The love we extend to others flows naturally from our love for God. It reflects our gratitude for the grace we have received through Jesus' life and sacrifice and expresses our desire to grow more like Him in every aspect of leadership.

Leading through service allows us to participate in the work of Christ in the world. When we do this, we model His compassion, humility, and willingness to put others first. This is the heart of Christian servant leadership and the enduring legacy we are called to embody as we guide, support, and care for those around us.

Prayer for Servant Leadership

Lord Jesus,
Thank You for showing us the true meaning of servant leadership through Your life, humility, and love. Shape our hearts so that we may lead as You led, not seeking status or recognition, but seeking to serve those You place in our care.
Give us wisdom in difficult decisions, courage when leadership is costly, and compassion for every person we encounter. Fill our workplaces with Your peace, and let our actions reflect Your character.

Strengthen us to love You with all our heart, soul, and mind, and to love our neighbors as ourselves. May our leadership honor You, point others toward Your grace, and bring hope to those who need it most. Guide us each day so that we may grow more like You in all that we do.
Amen.

Action Step 1: Begin Each Day by Inviting Christ to Shape Your Leadership

Take a few quiet moments at the start of the day to pray for humility, wisdom, and a heart that seeks to serve others. Ask God to guide your decisions, your conversations, and the way you respond to challenges.

Action Step 2: Choose One Practical Act of Humble Service Each Day

Look for a small, often unnoticed need in your workplace and meet it personally. This could include assisting a team member, offering encouragement, or stepping into a task others overlook. Let these actions form a habit of Christlike presence.

Action Step 3: Lead Difficult Conversations with Compassion and Clarity

When you face tough decisions or moments of conflict, practice transparency, empathy, and integrity. Prepare your heart ahead of time by asking God to help you honor both truth and grace in the way you communicate.

Action Step 4: Reflect Regularly on How Your Leadership Aligns with the Example of Jesus

At the end of the week, pause to consider where you embodied servant leadership and where you struggled. Invite the Holy Spirit to strengthen you and to shape your character more deeply in the image of Christ.

Reflection and Journal Prompts

1. Where in my current leadership role do I sense God inviting me to serve more intentionally? Reflect on specific relationships, responsibilities, or situations where a posture of Christlike service could make a meaningful difference.
2. When have I recently faced a difficult decision, and how did my approach reflect (or fall short of) the heart of Jesus? Write honestly about the tensions you navigated, the emotions you carried, and what you learned about yourself as a leader.
3. How do I respond when serving others is costly, inconvenient, or goes unnoticed? Consider what these moments reveal about your motivations, desires, and dependence on God, and how the Spirit might be shaping your character through them.
4. Who in my workplace or circle of influence needs encouragement, support, or compassion from me right now? Identify one person and reflect on how you can be present for them in a way that reflects Christ's love and humility.

Lesson 30

Create Safety in the Storm

Healthcare has always been demanding, but recent years have brought unprecedented challenges. Leaders at all levels often wear multiple hats because of staffing and financial constraints. The workload is heavy, and the pressure can take a serious toll. Staffing shortages, high turnover, employee grievances, patient complaints, regulatory demands, financial pressures, ethical dilemmas, and legal challenges all contribute to the strain. Frontline staff feel it most acutely as they manage heavier patient loads, extensive documentation, and rising expectations for quality care.

In addition, change is constant. Technological advancements, legislation, reimbursement changes, and shifting organizational priorities leave little time to adapt before the next wave arrives. Instead of simplifying work, each shift adds complexity and uncertainty, making healthcare one of the most demanding fields today.

In such an environment, it is difficult for anyone to feel safe. People long to hear words like, *"This too shall pass," "It's going to be okay," "Your position is secure,"* and *"We will get through this together."* These simple statements carry real weight. As Christian healthcare leaders, we are called to model this steady reassurance, creating a sense of safety and calm even in the midst of the storm.

Leading with Peace and Presence

Messages always flow from the top, whether hopeful or fearful, calming or chaotic. Whenever possible, choose to speak with hope. Be the leader who

DOI: 10.4324/9781003769781-33

is positive rather than pessimistic, supportive rather than critical, forgiving rather than harsh, encouraging rather than demanding, and reassuring rather than anxious. In doing so, you create safety in the storm. This is easier to do when we remember the power of God's presence:

> He stilled the storm to a whisper; the waves of the sea were hushed.
>
> Psalm 107:29 (NIV)

Leaders are called to reflect that same calming presence, offering peace when others feel overwhelmed. Crises come and go. Seasons of life change. No situation lasts forever. Even jobs come and go, and that's okay. What matters most is that God remains.

The best gift you can give to those you lead is to remind them of this truth: God is with them, and so are you. Stay steady. Stay encouraging. Stay reassuring. This matters far more than eloquent speeches, technical skill, regulatory expertise, or visionary plans. People will remember how you made them feel: safe, understood, and cared for.

You will not lead perfectly. None of us do. But every moment you choose peace over panic, compassion over frustration, and faith over fear is a moment to carry with quiet confidence. That is Jesus working in you and through you.

Jesus Calms the Storm

Few stories illustrate calm leadership better than the moment Jesus faced a storm with His disciples. One evening, as they crossed the Sea of Galilee, a fierce storm arose. Wind and waves battered the boat, and the disciples were terrified, fearing they would drown. Meanwhile, Jesus slept peacefully in the stern.

Frantic, they woke Him, saying, *"Teacher, don't you care if we drown?"* Jesus stood, spoke to the wind and waves, and immediately the storm ceased. The sea grew calm, and the disciples were left in awe, asking,

> Who is this? Even the wind and the waves obey Him!
>
> Mark 4:35–41 (NIV)

This story reminds us that God's presence brings calm amid chaos. The disciples' fear shows how overwhelming storms can feel. Yet when Jesus acted, fear turned to awe. They saw He was in control, even in the midst of turmoil.

As leaders, we may not be able to remove every challenge our team faces, but we can reflect His presence. Our calm, faith-filled responses guide others through uncertainty, providing stability, hope, and reassurance. Like the disciples, those we lead will notice and be transformed by our steadiness in the storm.

Pacing Change Wisely

Another way leaders create environments of safety is by managing the pace of change. Some issues are beyond a leader's control and must be addressed immediately. But often, leaders can choose how much to ask of their teams at a given time. A certain amount of change is manageable, but beyond that point, it becomes overwhelming.

The right pace depends on the nature of the change, the organization's resources, and the people involved. Wise leaders consider both the operational and emotional capacity of their teams. They meet regularly with team members, take time to know each person beyond their title or role, and create safe spaces for honest feedback, especially around workload and change fatigue.

Even so, there will be times when you must ask a great deal of your team. The workload may be heavy, the pace relentless, and the number of changes overwhelming. In these moments, it's important to acknowledge what people are feeling. Reassure them that their best will be enough and remind them that you will face the challenges together until calmer waters return.

When team members struggle visibly, you always have a choice in how you respond. You can meet them with understanding and empathy, or you can come across as cold and detached. Many leaders unintentionally choose the latter as a form of self-protection when they feel overwhelmed, anxious, or powerless. It can feel easier to turn off emotions and simply say, *"That's just the way it is."* But this is a mistake. It may protect you in the short term, but it erodes trust over time, and it is not Christlike leadership.

Providing Emotional Safety

In seasons of pressure, emotional safety becomes just as important as physical safety. People need to know they can speak openly, admit mistakes, and ask for help without fear of judgment or punishment. When leaders respond with patience and understanding, they build trust, and trust is the foundation of resilience.

Jesus often led this way. He welcomed questions, doubts, and even failures from His disciples. When Peter sank in the water, Jesus reached out His hand before offering correction. That same grace is what our teams need from us. They will make mistakes, grow tired, and sometimes lose hope. But if they know their leader sees them with compassion, they will find the courage to try again.

In my own leadership journey, I remember the leaders who made me feel safe and secure and those who did not. Those experiences were starkly different, and they are important to reflect on as we lead our own teams. As leaders, we always have the opportunity and responsibility to ensure our team members feel valued, supported, and safe.

Anchored in the Storm

Creating safety in the storm is not about removing every challenge. It is about how we, as leaders, show up when life feels overwhelming. It is about reflecting God's presence, speaking hope into fear, pacing change thoughtfully, and offering emotional safety to those entrusted to our care.

As Christian leaders, our influence is measured less by technical skill, policies, or plans, and more by the atmosphere we cultivate. People will remember how we made them feel. That is the lasting legacy of leadership rooted in faith.

Storms will come. Workloads will surge. Change will arrive faster than we can anticipate. Yet when we stay steady, compassionate, and anchored in God's presence, we create a refuge amid the turbulence. By modeling calm, hope, and empathy, we give our teams the courage to persevere and reflect Christ to the world through the way we lead.

Lead with faith. Lead with presence. Lead with peace. Lead with hope. The storm may rage, but God is with you, and so are those you lead. Together, you can navigate the waves, reach calmer waters, and thrive in the work He has called you to do.

Action Step 1: Speak Hope into Every Situation

Make it a daily practice to offer encouragement and reassurance to your team. Use words that affirm their value, acknowledge challenges, and emphasize that you are in it together. Even small statements like, "We'll get through this together," or "Your effort matters" can significantly reduce stress and build trust.

Action Step 2: Pace Change Thoughtfully

Before introducing new initiatives or shifts in workflow, assess your team's capacity. Prioritize changes, sequence them logically, and communicate clearly. Avoid overloading your team. Acknowledge the pressure when it exists and provide support to help them navigate transitions.

Action Step 3: Cultivate Emotional Safety

Create an environment where team members feel safe admitting mistakes, asking questions, or expressing concerns without fear of judgment. Listen actively, validate feelings, and respond with empathy. Your consistent compassion builds resilience and encourages openness.

Action Step 4: Model Steadfast Faith and Calm Presence

Anchor yourself in God's presence so that your demeanor reflects peace and stability. Your calm, faith-filled response to crises can set the tone for the entire team. Lead by example in showing patience, forgiveness, and hope, even when external pressures are high.

Reflection and Journal Prompts

1. Think about a recent stressful situation in your team or organization. How did your words, tone, and actions influence your team's sense of safety? What might you do differently next time to reflect calm, faith, and reassurance?
2. List the major changes or challenges your team is currently facing. Which ones can you pace thoughtfully, and which are beyond your control? How can you help your team navigate these pressures without feeling overwhelmed?

3. Reflect on your team's environment: Do people feel safe to share concerns, admit mistakes, or ask for help? What steps can you take to strengthen trust and create a culture of emotional safety?
4. Consider your own reliance on God in times of stress. How does your faith guide your leadership in difficult situations? In what ways can you intentionally model trust, hope, and peace for your team this week?

IV LEADING THROUGH PRESSURE AND CHANGE

Lesson 31

Cultivate a Peaceful Presence

The best leaders seem to radiate a peaceful presence, regardless of circumstances. When others bring anxiety, overwhelm, or concern, those feelings begin to fade as they are shared. Rather than judgment, there is understanding. What emerges instead is calm, trust, strength, and a quiet reassurance that things will be okay. These leaders truly listen and help others find a path forward. You never feel like you are facing challenges alone.

Encountering a leader like this is powerful. They create a sense of personal and professional safety. Even when mistakes occur, their grace, encouragement, and steady support create a remarkably strong bond. These are the leaders we long to work for, and with intention, we can become this kind of leader ourselves.

In healthcare, this kind of presence is urgently needed. Burnout remains high due to workforce shortages, heavy workloads, and constant scrutiny. Judgment and criticism are common, and providers often carry the weight of potential harm. This includes psychological and physical harm, as healthcare environments involve ongoing risks of verbal, emotional, and physical abuse. It also includes threats related to litigation, reputation, regulatory surveys, and accreditation challenges. These pressures affect clinicians, administrators, and senior leaders alike, making a calm and reassuring presence more essential than ever.

DOI: 10.4324/9781003769781-35

Cultivating a Peaceful Presence in Scripture

The qualities of a leader who radiates peace are deeply reflected in Scripture. The Bible repeatedly calls leaders to act with gentleness, patience, and humility, creating environments where others feel safe and valued. We are reminded of this in Proverbs:

> A gentle answer turns away wrath, but a harsh word stirs up anger.
>
> Proverbs 15:1 (NIV)

Leaders who cultivate a calm and understanding presence live out this principle. By choosing gentleness over harshness, they diffuse tension and build trust within their teams. Jesus Himself provides the ultimate example of a peaceful presence. In His interactions, He listened, responded with compassion, and offered reassurance even in difficult circumstances. In Matthew 11:28–30, He invites those who are weary to find rest in Him, demonstrating a presence that brings comfort and safety:

> Come to me, all you who are weary and burdened, and I will give you rest. Take my yoke upon you and learn from me, for I am gentle and humble in heart, and you will find rest for your souls. For my yoke is easy and my burden is light.
>
> Matthew 11:28–30 (NIV)

Leaders who follow this example bring calm to stressful situations and offer hope, trust, and encouragement to those they serve. Scripture also points us to the fruit of the Spirit in Galatians 5:22–23: love, joy, peace, patience, kindness, goodness, faithfulness, gentleness, and self-control. These qualities provide a framework for leaders seeking to cultivate a peaceful presence. By embodying them, leaders offer stability and reassurance, helping others feel supported and valued even in the most challenging environments.

Practical Steps for Leaders

- **Respond with gentleness**
  When tensions arise, answer calmly and thoughtfully to diffuse conflict rather than escalate it.

- **Listen with compassion**
  Truly hear the concerns of your team, creating an environment where people feel safe to share.
- **Model the fruit of the Spirit**
  Demonstrate love, patience, kindness, and self-control in daily interactions to build trust and stability.
- **Provide reassurance and guidance**
  Offer support when mistakes happen and help your team develop plans to move forward together.
- **Maintain calm under pressure**
  Use prayer, reflection, and reliance on God to keep your presence peaceful, especially in high-stress situations.
- **Encourage and uplift**
  Celebrate successes, affirm efforts, and remind your team that they are valued and supported, especially during challenging seasons.

Mindfulness Practices

Leaders can also cultivate a peaceful presence through mindfulness practices. Some of these have been mentioned before, but they are worth repeating here. These include:

- **Pause before responding**
  Take a breath before reacting to stressful situations or difficult conversations.
- **Practice deep breathing**
  Use slow, intentional breaths to calm your body and mind when tension arises.
- **Reflect daily**
  Spend a few minutes each day reviewing interactions and considering how to respond with calm and understanding.
- **Prayer and meditation**
  Integrate time with God into your day to center yourself and seek guidance.
- **Body awareness**
  Notice tension in your body and consciously relax your shoulders, jaw, and posture.

- **Gratitude journaling**
  Record things you are thankful for to maintain perspective and emotional balance.
- **Active listening**
  Focus fully on the person speaking, letting go of distractions and judgments.
- **Mindful transitions**
  Take a short pause between tasks or meetings to reset your mindset.
- **Visualization**
  Imagine yourself responding calmly and compassionately in challenging situations before they happen.
- **Limit multitasking**
  Focus on one task or conversation at a time to reduce stress and increase presence.
- **Use guided meditations or mindfulness apps**
  Leverage apps or recordings for daily guided meditation, visualization, and deep breathing exercises to help maintain focus, calm, and emotional balance.

Progress Over Perfection

Even with these tools and the best intentions, every leader is only human. When mistakes occur, it is important not to see them as failures. Instead, view them as small, temporary dips from which you can recover.

Consistency and determination are what build lasting change. Over time, old patterns can be broken, and new habits formed until they become almost automatic. Cultivating a peaceful presence works in the same way. Each time you respond with calm and understanding, it reinforces this habit and strengthens your ability to lead with peace.

A peaceful presence doesn't happen by accident. It takes daily effort, and structure can help. This might include grounding yourself in Scripture before work, practicing a short meditation over lunch, or planning mindful transitions throughout the day. There are many ways to integrate these practices into your personal and professional life. Ultimately, it comes down to intention and the choices we prioritize.

The effort is worth it. A peaceful presence transforms both us and those we serve. Now more than ever, we need peace in our lives. The world can feel dark at times, but a peaceful presence becomes a ray of light. Letting that light shine reflects Jesus working within us. Every small moment in which we respond with calm and clarity matters. We may not always see the results, but they matter deeply. In the end, life comes down to these moments, and we have the opportunity to make each one count.

Action Step 1: Pause and Respond with Intention

Before reacting to stressful situations or difficult conversations, take a deep breath and intentionally choose a calm, understanding response.

Action Step 2: Integrate Daily Mindfulness Practices

Use tools such as guided meditation, deep breathing, prayer, or mindful transitions to center yourself and maintain clarity throughout the day.

Action Step 3: Model the Fruit of the Spirit

Actively demonstrate love, patience, kindness, gentleness, and self-control in your interactions to build trust and a stable environment for your team.

Action Step 4: Reflect and Learn from Moments of Humanness

When you lose your calm or respond imperfectly, treat it as a temporary dip rather than failure, and commit to returning to a peaceful, intentional presence.

Reflection and Journal Prompts

1. Reflect on situations or interactions that tend to disrupt your peace. What patterns do you notice, and how can you prepare to respond more calmly in the future?

2. Think about a recent interaction where you felt you were able to remain calm and supportive. What specific behaviors or attitudes helped you maintain a peaceful presence?
3. Consider the verses from Proverbs 15:1, Matthew 11:28–30, and Galatians 5:22–23. How can these Scriptures guide your responses and attitude in leadership today?
4. Write down one or two practical steps you will take this week to intentionally cultivate a peaceful presence, such as a mindfulness practice, intentional pause, or modeling a fruit of the Spirit in a challenging situation.

Lesson 32

Shine as a Beacon of Hope

In previous chapters, we've explored the importance of leaders spreading hope. In this lesson, we'll look more deeply at what that truly means. Christian leaders are called to be beacons of hope, steady lights that guide others through uncertainty, exhaustion, and fear.

In healthcare today, hope is like light breaking through darkness. People are drawn to it instinctively, sometimes desperately. For many clinicians, managers, and leaders, hope feels like coming up for air after nearly drowning. It is a deep breath of life and renewal that reminds them they can keep going.

The Weight of the Work

This is not an exaggeration. While some days may feel manageable, the ongoing pressures of healthcare can create a slow, steady fatigue that builds over time. Without renewal, that fatigue can settle into despair and spiritual dryness. It can feel like walking through the valley of the shadow of death, where purpose and joy fade and burnout takes root.

Much of this burden comes from moral injury, the hidden pain that arises when people cannot act in accordance with their values or provide the care they know is needed. In this environment, people need more than motivation. They need meaning and hope.

DOI: 10.4324/9781003769781-36

Paul and Silas: Hope in the Midst of Trials

The Bible provides powerful examples of hope in the midst of difficulty. Consider Paul and Silas in Philippi. After being unjustly beaten and imprisoned, they were placed in stocks in the inner prison, with no hope of immediate release. Yet in the darkness of that night, they prayed and sang hymns to God. Their hope and faith did not waver, even in chains and uncertainty.

Suddenly, an earthquake shook the prison, opening the doors and loosening the chains of every prisoner. Their steadfast hope and trust in God became a light for others. Even the jailer, who witnessed their faith and joy, was transformed. This story reminds us that hope is not passive. It is a steady, active trust that God is present, even when circumstances feel impossible.

As Christian leaders, we are called to be like Paul and Silas in our workplaces. Even when resources are scarce, workloads are heavy, and challenges seem insurmountable, our faith, encouragement, and example can inspire those around us. Hope is contagious, and the light of one steadfast leader can illuminate the darkest night for an entire team.

Practical Ways to Be a Beacon of Hope

The following are concrete ways we can foster hope in our teams, even amid the pressures of healthcare:

- **Speak Words That Encourage and Inspire**
  Hope is often conveyed through what we say. Simple, sincere words can make a profound difference. A timely "I see your effort, and it really matters," or "We will get through this together," reminds people they are not alone. Speak with positivity, avoiding fear-driven or overly critical messages. Your words carry authority, shaping not just policies, but the emotional climate of your team.
- **Celebrate Small Wins**
  In an environment where challenges can feel endless, recognizing progress matters. Celebrate small victories: a patient safely discharged, a team member stepping up, or a workflow improvement. These moments reinforce that work is meaningful and that each contribution counts. Celebration fuels hope more than abstract promises ever can.

- **Model Resilience and Faith**
  Teams look to their leaders not just for guidance, but for emotional cues. Demonstrating calm, steady faith in difficult situations reassures your team that challenges can be faced and overcome. By acknowledging difficulties while maintaining perspective, your actions teach hope more effectively than words alone.
- **Build Personal Connections**
  Hope grows in relationships. Take time to know your team members as people, not just roles. Listen actively, ask about their struggles, and show genuine concern. Even brief, meaningful interactions communicate that each individual matters and that their work has value beyond metrics and reports.
- **Encourage Renewal and Rest**
  Hope cannot flourish in constant exhaustion. Advocate for rest, self-care, and professional growth. Encourage team members to take breaks, access spiritual or emotional support, and engage in activities that renew their sense of purpose. Supporting renewal is a tangible way to sustain hope.
- **Connect Work to Meaning and Calling**
  Remind your team that their work has eternal significance. Healthcare is a ministry of service, reflecting Christ's compassion and care. When people see the impact of their work on patients' lives, families, and communities, hope is renewed. Encourage reflection on why each role matters, connecting daily tasks to the larger mission of faithful service.

Anchoring Hope in Scripture

As we focus on concrete ways to spread hope to others, it can be helpful to reflect on related passages from Scripture:

> May the God of hope fill you with all joy and peace as you trust in him, so that you may overflow with hope by the power of the Holy Spirit.
>
> Romans 15:13 (NIV)

Reflect on how your own hope, rooted in God, can naturally overflow to those you lead.

> But those who hope in the Lord will renew their strength. They will soar on wings like eagles; they will run and not grow weary, they will walk and not be faint.
>
> Isaiah 40:31 (NIV)

Consider how anchoring yourself in God can help you sustain energy and perseverance, even in the most demanding environments.

> Let us hold unswervingly to the hope we profess, for he who promised is faithful.
>
> Hebrews 10:23 (NIV)

Reflect on how steadfast hope in God's promises can guide both your decisions and the tone you set for your team.

Shining Light Through the Challenges

Being a beacon of hope takes intentionality, empathy, and courage. Leaders who prioritize it do more than manage tasks. They cultivate an environment where people feel empowered. In doing so, hope spreads like light, guiding teams through challenges, exhaustion, and uncertainty. As you reflect on these principles and passages, consider how you can let your light shine today, sharing hope with those around you, even in the most challenging moments.

Action Step 1: Speak Hope into the Day

Start each day by intentionally sharing words of encouragement with your team. Acknowledge their efforts, highlight achievements, and remind them of the bigger purpose behind their work. Even brief affirmations can shift the emotional climate.

Action Step 2: Celebrate Progress, Big and Small

Take note of small victories such as successful patient outcomes, workflow improvements, or moments of teamwork. Share these wins publicly with your team to reinforce that their work is meaningful and valued.

Action Step 3: Demonstrate Faith and Resilience

Model calm, steady faith in challenging situations. Show your team how to face difficulties with perspective, trust, and hope. Let your own example teach perseverance more than words alone could.

Action Step 4: Foster Renewal and Connection

Encourage rest, personal care, and spiritual renewal. Take time to connect personally with team members, listen to their struggles, and affirm their value. Creating space for both emotional and spiritual refreshment helps sustain hope over the long term.

Reflection and Journal Prompts

1. Reflect on what renews your hope and sustains you as a leader. How can you draw on God's presence to maintain your perspective and energy, even during the most challenging days?
2. Think about the last week: how have your words influenced the mood and morale of your team? What specific things can you say or do to intentionally spread hope in the coming week?
3. Consider the small victories your team has achieved recently. How can you better notice and celebrate these moments to remind your team that their work is meaningful?
4. Reflect on a time when your calm, faith-filled response encouraged others during a difficult situation. What lessons did you learn from that experience, and how can you apply them to create a culture of hope consistently?

Lesson 33

Be Positive and Encouraging

It may sound obvious, but being positive is essential for healthcare leaders in today's challenging environment. At the same time, positivity is not about being fake. It is a conscious choice in how we think, speak, and lead.

This practice is a form of mental conditioning. When we repeatedly run negative patterns in our minds, we reinforce discouragement and exhaustion. The more we focus on what is wrong, the more our outlook narrows and our energy declines. The opposite is also true. When we intentionally focus on what is right, we strengthen habits of resilience and optimism. Over time, this becomes a part of who we are and shapes the emotional climate around us.

Positivity in leadership does not mean ignoring problems. It means approaching challenges with a mindset that believes solutions are possible and that people can rise to meet them. It means choosing generosity over criticism and words that build rather than diminish. In healthcare settings, where people are often stretched thin, these small choices can have a powerful impact on morale, teamwork, and well-being.

Scripture on Encouragement

As Christian healthcare leaders, we can reflect on the following passages from Scripture as we seek to model encouragement in our leadership.

> Therefore encourage one another and build each other up, just as in fact you are doing.
>
> 1 Thessalonians 5:11 (NIV)

DOI: 10.4324/9781003769781-37

Paul wrote these words to a young church facing persecution, uncertainty, and discouragement about the future. His goal was to strengthen their faith, comfort them, and remind them of the hope they have in Christ. In the same way, we can encourage our teams as they navigate uncertainty and discouragement in their work.

> And let us consider how we may spur one another on toward love and good deeds, not giving up meeting together, as some are in the habit of doing, but encouraging one another.
>
> Hebrews 10:24–25 (NIV)

Hebrews was written to believers who were weary and under significant pressure. Many faced social rejection, persecution, and the temptation to return to familiar practices that felt safer. The author writes to strengthen their endurance and point them toward faithfulness in Christ. This passage reminds us to encourage our teams toward loving actions, meaningful work, and mutual support, especially when morale is low.

> Anxiety weighs down the heart, but a kind word cheers it up.
>
> Proverbs 12:25 (NIV)

This simple yet powerful proverb highlights the impact of our words. Kindness and encouragement can ease anxiety and lift heavy hearts. For Christian healthcare leaders, this small daily practice can be transformational for teams struggling with stress and overwhelm.

Scripture on Guarding Your Mindset

Scripture also offers guidance as we consider our mindset and the habits that shape our thinking.

> Finally, brothers and sisters, whatever is true, whatever is noble, whatever is right, whatever is pure, whatever is lovely, whatever is admirable, if anything is excellent or praiseworthy, think about such things.
>
> Philippians 4:8 (NIV)

As Christians, we are called to practice this intentionally in both our personal and professional lives. Just as what we eat affects our physical health, the thoughts we dwell on influence our spiritual and mental well-being. While thoughts may arise uninvited, we can choose which ones we nurture and reinforce. We also have influence over the information, entertainment, music, and reading we consume. Whenever possible, it is wise to make a conscious choice to focus on what is pure, noble, and true.

Scripture on Speaking Life

When we talk about being positive and encouraging, we are really talking about speaking life. The following passages are especially powerful as we think about this in a healthcare context.

> Gracious words are a honeycomb, sweet to the soul and healing to the bones.
>
> Proverbs 16:24 (NIV)

This verse reminds us that a leader's words carry real influence. They affect people mentally, physically, and spiritually. Through our words we can foster healing, ease stress, and strengthen resilience, bringing comfort and renewal.

> Do not let any unwholesome talk come out of your mouths, but only what is helpful for building others up according to their needs, that it may benefit those who listen.
>
> Ephesians 4:29 (NIV)

This passage echoes the familiar wisdom that if our words are not helpful, it is best not to speak at all. For Christian leaders, this is a call to intentional speech. To speak life and reflect Christ at work within us, our words should build, encourage, and meet the needs of those who hear them. When our speech uplifts others, it becomes a powerful expression of leadership and care.

Practical Application for Healthcare Leaders

Putting positivity and encouragement into practice does not have to be complicated. The following strategies offer concrete ways to bring these principles to life in daily leadership.

- **Celebrate Small Wins**
  Acknowledge even minor achievements to reinforce progress and build morale.
- **Use Encouraging Language**
  Speak words that uplift, guide, and motivate, especially during stressful moments.
- **Model Hope and Joy**
  Demonstrate resilience and optimism under pressure. Your attitude sets the emotional tone for the team.
- **Check in Personally**
  Take brief, intentional moments to listen, encourage, and affirm individual efforts.
- **Focus on Strengths**
  Highlight abilities and successes rather than dwelling on mistakes or shortcomings.
- **Create a Culture of Sharing**
  Encourage team members to recognize and support one another. Collective encouragement multiplies its impact.

The Power of Positivity in Leadership

Being positive and encouraging is more than a leadership strategy. It is a choice, a discipline, and a reflection of Christ's character in action. When we live this out, we create a ripple effect that strengthens teams, builds resilience, and deepens trust.

Scripture reminds us that encouragement, hope, and kindness are not optional. They are central to how we care for one another and cultivate healthy communities. From celebrating small wins to offering gracious words, these daily actions shape a culture where people feel supported and strengthened.

This influence extends far beyond operations and outcomes. The way we communicate and the spirit we carry shape the emotional and spiritual climate of our organizations. By choosing encouragement and optimism, we help others persevere through difficult seasons and create environments where teams can truly flourish.

Action Step 1: Recognize Achievements Daily

Make it a habit to notice and acknowledge both small and large successes. A simple word of praise or public recognition reinforces progress and fosters a culture of encouragement.

Action Step 2: Speak Life

Consciously use language that uplifts, motivates, and guides. Avoid criticism or negative talk, and focus on helping others grow through constructive, affirming communication.

Action Step 3: Model Hope and Resilience

During challenging moments, demonstrate calm, optimism, and faith in solutions. Your attitude sets the tone for the team and encourages them to persevere with confidence.

Action Step 4: Engage Personally with Team Members

Take time to connect individually with team members. Listen to their concerns, celebrate their efforts, and offer words of encouragement. Personal attention shows you value them as people, not just as employees.

Reflection and Journal Prompts

1. How often do I consciously choose to focus on what is good, true, and uplifting in my work and interactions? Where do I notice negative patterns creeping in, and how can I reframe them?
2. What recent situation shows how my words either encouraged or discouraged someone on my team? What could I have said differently to build them up? How did my words affect the outcome or the person's morale?

3. In times of stress or uncertainty, how do I typically respond? What can I do to model calm, optimism, and hope for my team more consistently?
4. Who on my team might need encouragement right now, and what specific action or words can I offer them this week? How can I make encouragement a regular, intentional part of my leadership practice?

Lesson 34

Lead with Vision

Many leaders use the words calling, purpose, and vision. Yet each represents a distinct aspect of God's design for your life and work. Understanding these differences can help you lead with greater clarity, focus, and intention.

Calling—Why Am I Here?

Calling is God's invitation, rooted in His plan for your life. It is the reason you are in your field or role. In healthcare, for example, calling may draw you to the profession and sustain you through stress, setbacks, or burnout. Calling is foundational. It is received, not earned.

Purpose—What Am I Here to Do?

Purpose flows from your calling and gives it direction. It helps you see how your unique gifts, talents, and experiences can serve God and others in your current context. While calling gives the "why," purpose clarifies the "what" and "how" of your daily work. Purpose is actionable and practical. It gives your leadership and service shape and focus.

DOI: 10.4324/9781003769781-38

Vision—Where Are We Going?

Vision builds on calling and purpose by projecting a picture of the future that inspires and mobilizes others. As a leader, vision articulates a shared hope, a better tomorrow, and a clear direction for your team or organization. Vision turns your calling and purpose into a collective journey that others can understand, embrace, and contribute to. In short:

- **Calling** is God's invitation for your life.
- **Purpose** is how you live out that calling in your work.
- **Vision** is the future you seek to create as you lead others.

When calling, purpose, and vision align, you lead with clarity, confidence, and courage. You not only serve with faithfulness but also inspire those around you to follow God's plan for their lives. This distinction becomes clearer when we see it lived out in practice.

Putting Principles into Practice: A Leadership Example

Calling—Why Am I Here?

James, a hospital administrator, felt early in his career that God had placed him in healthcare to make a meaningful difference. He wasn't just interested in job titles or advancement. He sensed a deeper calling to serve patients and staff faithfully. That sense of calling gave him resilience during long hours, regulatory pressures, and emotionally difficult situations. Even when no one acknowledged his efforts, he knew his work had significance beyond recognition. It was part of God's plan.

Purpose—What Am I Here to Do?

As James continued in his role, he clarified his purpose: to create a hospital environment where both patients and staff could thrive. He implemented programs for staff well-being, improved patient safety protocols, and fostered a culture of compassion and accountability. Purpose gave him concrete direction, translating his calling into actionable initiatives that tangibly improved care and support for those around him.

Vision—Where Are We Going?

Building on his calling and purpose, James developed a vision for the hospital: a fully integrated care model that prioritized holistic well-being and empowered staff to provide compassionate, efficient care. He shared this vision at staff meetings, board presentations, and community events, painting a picture of a future where the hospital could serve as a model for excellence, safety, and faith-driven leadership. The vision inspired his team to move beyond routine tasks, aligning their daily efforts with a shared goal bigger than any individual role.

From Calling to Vision: My Leadership Journey

For part of my leadership journey, I was called to serve in long-term care and aging services. That calling led me to the nonprofit sector and to mission-driven organizations. My purpose emerged through the national culture change movement in aging services, a shift from institutional nursing homes to true, person-centered homes. This meant honoring residents' autonomy, choice, and dignity while redesigning environments to feel like home rather than a hospital.

In time, I helped lead the transformation of two continuing care retirement communities and their skilled nursing centers. This work was challenging. Regulations controlled nearly every aspect of care and facility design. To move forward, we needed a clear vision, one that was not just mine but shared by leadership, staff, residents, families, and community partners.

Large-scale transformation is never simple. It requires reexamining mission, culture, and values. It demands communication, collaboration, courage, and perseverance. Things sometimes do not go as planned, but the process itself becomes a powerful act of leadership and faithfulness.

Vision Is Never Formed Alone

My first exposure to this vision came during my master's practicum at a large Catholic health system. The CEO of the senior living division planted the first seeds in my mind. After the practicum, I stayed on for a time to support the Senior Vice President of Mission Integration, which allowed me to see how mission and innovation work together in leadership.

After completing my master's, I entered an Administrator-in-Training (AIT) program required to become a licensed nursing home administrator. I completed this program at a different faith-based, multi-site organization. My preceptor there was deeply committed to the culture change movement. During that experience, he helped me understand the model more fully and later hired me into my first administrator role. Together, we implemented operational and physical changes across two campuses.

Along the way, I continued learning from national and state professional associations, nonprofit leaders, consultants, and early adopters shaping this movement. I also completed two back-to-back, year-long leadership fellowships with my state and national aging services associations. These experiences allowed me to learn from some of the best leaders in the country and tour their campuses. When I eventually stepped into a CEO role, I continued leading these efforts, but always as part of a larger story that preceded me and would continue beyond me.

I share this because the word "vision" can make it sound as though leaders must create something entirely on their own. In reality, the best leaders are lifelong learners and collaborators. They listen, study innovations, learn from others, and work with their teams to shape and refine a shared vision.

Anchoring Vision in God's Guidance

It is important to recognize God's place in this process. While I continued learning from others, I also remained grounded in my walk with Him. I prayed about my desire to make a positive difference in the lives of others, asking God to guide my steps and help me pursue work that truly mattered. I remained open to His plans, seeking discernment for the best path forward for my organization. Scripture also provided guidance for shaping this strategy. As leaders, we may shape plans and articulate vision, but ultimately we walk by faith, trusting God to direct our steps. As Proverbs 3:5–6 reminds us:

> Trust in the Lord with all your heart and lean not on your own understanding; in all your ways submit to him, and he will make your paths straight.
>
> Proverbs 3:5–6 (NIV)

The Importance of Humility in Vision

Even when leaders act with the best intentions in shaping vision, we must remember that our perspective is limited. With experience comes wisdom, and wisdom reminds us that sometimes we are not entirely right. Plans that seem clear can have unintended consequences, and what we assume to be fear-based resistance may hold valuable insight.

This is why humility is essential in leadership. Especially in senior roles, it can be tempting to believe that vision gives us greater clarity than others. Yet humility calls us to slow down, listen, and involve the people most affected by change. Their perspective is not an obstacle to overcome, but a gift to be discerned. Humility does not weaken vision. It refines it.

Leading Vision with Humility and Hope

In the end, leadership is not about having all the answers or seeing the entire path ahead. The best leaders are faithful stewards. They are collaborators, learners, and communicators, willing to listen to God and to those He has placed around them. As you reflect on your own calling, purpose, and vision, do not walk alone. Seek counsel from trusted mentors and colleagues, and involve your team in the process.

Most importantly, stay close to God. Vision rooted in prayer is sustained by His wisdom, not our certainty. Keep asking Him to guide your steps, align your plans with His will, and shape a future that brings hope, healing, and glory to His name. Leadership grounded in calling, lived with purpose, and guided by God's vision is more than strategy. It is an act of faithfulness.

Action Step 1: Clarify Your Calling

Take time to consider where God is inviting you. Ask yourself: *Is there a direction or opportunity He may be guiding me toward? How can I discern His plan for my next steps?* Journal, pray, and seek counsel from trusted mentors to help identify where your calling may be leading you, whether in your current role or toward a new path God is inviting you to.

Action Step 2: Define Your Purpose

Identify the concrete ways your gifts, skills, and experiences serve others. Ask: *What specific actions can I take to live out my calling today? How does my work make a difference?* Create a short list of daily or weekly practices that reflect how you can serve others in this season.

Action Step 3: Develop and Communicate Vision

Envision the future you hope to create in your team or organization. Ask: *Where are we going? What difference will our collective efforts make?* Share this vision with colleagues, invite feedback, and refine it collaboratively.

Action Step 4: Lead with Humility and Faith

Recognize that leadership is a journey of learning, listening, and trusting God. Ask: *Am I staying open to counsel, feedback, and God's guidance?* Practice prayerful reflection, seek mentorship, and involve others in shaping and executing your vision.

Reflection and Journal Prompts

1. What experiences in your career or life have made you feel most aligned with God's guidance or invitation for your life? How do these moments inform your understanding of your calling?
2. In what ways are you currently living out your calling? Are there areas where your daily actions could better reflect the ways God is inviting you to serve?
3. Imagine the ideal outcome of your leadership or work. What does that future look like, and how does it serve others? How can you begin taking steps toward that vision today?
4. Reflect on a time when listening to others or seeking God's guidance changed your perspective or decision. How can you incorporate humility and faith more intentionally in your leadership moving forward?

Lesson 35

Prioritize Collaboration

One of the most important skills for leaders is collaboration. This is especially true in healthcare, which is marked by constant change, complex systems, and shared responsibility. In this environment, no one person has the knowledge or ability to meet every challenge. As a result, leaders must learn to rely on the wisdom, experience, and insight of others. As Scripture reminds us:

> Plans fail for lack of counsel, but with many advisers they succeed.
> Proverbs 15:22 (NIV)

As leaders grow in responsibility, the need for collaboration only deepens. It requires empowering team members, removing barriers, securing needed resources, and building trust. It also means prioritizing the holistic well-being of the people entrusted to your care.

Collaboration: Barriers and Best Practices

Collaboration requires intention, presence, and a careful awareness of human dynamics. Leaders can unintentionally undermine collaboration by leaning too far in either direction, being too hands-off or overly controlling. Both extremes erode trust, engagement, and effectiveness. Too little guidance leaves teams uncertain about expectations and priorities, while too much control stifles initiative and diminishes professional judgment. In

DOI: 10.4324/9781003769781-39

either case, the result is the same: reduced collaboration, frustration, and wasted energy.

True collaborative leadership exists in balance. It calls for presence without domination, clarity without rigidity, and shared decision-making that honors professional expertise. Leaders who cultivate collaboration demonstrate respect for autonomy, communicate transparently, and create an environment of psychological safety where team members can contribute fully without fear of criticism or reprisal. The difference often comes down to the habits leaders practice daily.

Practices that Weaken Collaboration

Leaders can teach us in both positive and negative ways. Observing poor leadership reveals behaviors that undermine collaboration and erode trust, including:

- **Making decisions in isolation**
  Acting without input from those affected often leads to poor outcomes and frustrated teams.
- **Assuming all the answers**
  Leaders who position themselves as the "smartest person in the room" shut down creativity, honesty, and shared problem-solving.
- **Ignoring frontline expertise**
  Overlooking the insight of those closest to the work signals a lack of respect and produces solutions that may not hold up in practice.
- **Communicating decisions without context**
  Failing to explain the "why" behind choices breeds confusion, resistance, and suspicion.
- **Micromanaging highly trained professionals**
  Excessive control stifles initiative and erodes confidence, especially in fields where autonomy is essential.
- **Dismissing concerns or differing perspectives**
  When people feel unheard, they disengage and valuable information is lost.
- **Prioritizing hierarchy over humanity**
  Using rank or authority to force compliance damages relationships and reduces collaboration to mere obligation.

- **Withholding resources or support**
  Leaders who do not advocate for their teams hinder performance and reduce trust.
- **Failing to recognize contributions**
  Overlooking or minimizing teamwork weakens morale and diminishes shared ownership.
- **Overlooking capacity and workload**
  Assigning more responsibilities than people can realistically manage leads to burnout and frustration.
- **Creating unnecessary complexity**
  Rigid or convoluted processes waste time and distract from meaningful work.
- **Using fear or punitive measures**
  Threatening, shaming, or punishing team members erodes trust and psychological safety.

Practices That Strengthen Collaboration

Recognizing what to avoid is only the first step. Equally important is adopting behaviors that build trust and engagement including:

- **Engaging stakeholders early**
  Inviting input at the start of decisions or projects so people feel included and solutions are better informed.
- **Cultivating a learning posture**
  Approaching situations with curiosity, humility, and a willingness to be influenced by others' expertise.
- **Seeking frontline insight**
  Regularly asking those closest to the work what they see, what is working, and what needs attention.
- **Communicating clearly and transparently**
  Sharing decisions along with the reasoning behind them to build trust and alignment.
- **Empowering rather than micromanaging**
  Providing clarity, support, and resources, then giving people the space they need to apply their skills effectively.

- **Listening deeply to concerns and perspectives**
  Creating an environment where people feel safe to share honestly and responding with respect and openness.
- **Leading relationally, not just positionally**
  Building authentic relationships marked by trust, compassion, and mutual respect.
- **Respecting capacity and workload**
  Ensuring responsibilities are realistic, providing training when roles change, and removing unnecessary barriers.
- **Simplifying processes where possible**
  Streamlining requirements and procedures to focus on what truly matters, reducing wasted effort and frustration.
- **Advocating for your team**
  Protecting their time, securing resources, removing barriers, and celebrating their accomplishments.
- **Promoting psychological safety**
  Encouraging open dialogue, safe feedback, and honest expression of ideas without fear of retribution.
- **Celebrating shared wins**
  Recognizing and affirming the contributions of the team to strengthen commitment and reinforce a collaborative culture.

Leading Like Jesus: Collaboration in Action

For Christian healthcare leaders, these lessons take on added depth. Leadership is not just about efficiency or outcomes. It is a reflection of Christ's love, humility, and service. Relationship dynamics matter deeply, and the way we lead can either build up or discourage those around us.

Jesus Himself modeled collaborative leadership. He called the apostles to join Him in His work, empowering them to share His message of hope and healing. Likewise, we are called to work alongside others, with humility, patience, and care. When we embrace collaboration in this way, we enable team members to grow into their best selves, advance the mission of our organizations, and foster a culture of trust. True Christian leadership flourishes when we lead not for recognition or control, but with a servant's heart, partnering with others to make a lasting impact.

Action Step 1: Engage Your Team Regularly

Schedule consistent check-ins, meetings, or touchpoints to ensure voices are heard and ideas are shared early in decision-making.

Action Step 2: Promote Shared Decision-Making

Involve team members in planning and problem-solving to foster ownership, trust, and better outcomes.

Action Step 3: Build Psychological Safety

Create an environment where team members can speak openly, share concerns, and offer suggestions without fear of criticism or retribution.

Action Step 4: Lead with a Servant's Heart

Prioritize relationships, remove barriers, provide resources, and celebrate the contributions of your team, modeling humility, care, and encouragement.

Reflection and Journal Prompts

1. Reflect on a recent project or decision: How did you engage others? Did you listen actively, involve the right people, and balance guidance with autonomy? What would you do differently next time?
2. Consider your team's dynamics: Are there any behaviors, processes, or patterns that hinder collaboration? How might you address these while maintaining trust and respect?
3. Think about the ways your leadership supports or unintentionally undermines team members' growth and well-being. How can you adjust your approach to better empower and uplift others?
4. Reflect on Jesus' example of servant leadership and collaboration. How can you emulate His humility, patience, and encouragement in your interactions with your team this week?

Lesson 36

Discern Before You Decide

Healthcare leaders make serious decisions every day, often under pressure and with imperfect options. Situations can be complex, resources scarce, and authority limited, even for senior leaders. Yet the work must go on, and the choices leaders make affect not only the organization but also the well-being of patients, staff, and colleagues. The good news is that Christian healthcare leaders do not have to face these decisions alone. By seeking God's wisdom, they can exercise faithful and grounded judgment. As Scripture reminds us:

> If any of you lacks wisdom, you should ask God, who gives generously to all without finding fault, and it will be given to you.
>
> James 1:5 (NIV)

One way to do this is by pausing when faced with an important decision. While some situations require immediate action, others allow time for reflection. When possible, pause to reflect, gather counsel from others, and bring the decision before God in prayer. Discernment takes practice, but over time it forms leaders who respond thoughtfully rather than reactively.

Listening for God's Response

When you have asked God for wisdom, the next step is to listen for His response. This requires stillness, reflection, and intention. We live in an era of constant pressure where answers are expected immediately. Yet even a

DOI: 10.4324/9781003769781-40

single evening of quiet reflection can have a meaningful impact on your decisions and on those affected by them.

We must intentionally create this kind of space for God to be part of our leadership and our lives. These moments are sacred, and when we invite God in, we open ourselves to guidance that goes beyond our own understanding. In that quiet, we may gain clarity, discernment, or a gentle confirmation of the path before us.

The Process of Discernment

In moments of silence, contemplation of Scripture can be deeply helpful. It does not have to be lengthy. The practice itself is what matters most. During this time, guidance may come through the words you are reading or through the quiet prompting of the Holy Spirit.

Through prayer, we not only ask for wisdom but also release our burdens to God. This can bring immense relief as we sense His strength and support. When we feel His presence, it reminds us that we are never alone. He is always by our side.

God may also speak through others He has placed in our lives, so listen attentively to wise counsel. This guidance may come from people of faith, team members at work, or those you least expect. By valuing every individual who comes into our lives, we remain open to God's wisdom.

The amount of time required for discernment will vary based on the issue at hand. Sometimes it may be brief. Even then, turning to God creates space for His guidance to take root in your heart. In urgent moments, it can be as simple as asking, "What would Jesus do?" Consider how He might approach the decision before you and let that guide your actions when time is short.

It is also important to reflect on acceptance. When we seek God's guidance, clarity may come quickly, or it may not. Trust that your prayers have been heard. God knows your sincerity and your heart. Sometimes there is no easy solution or perfect path forward, and that may be what God is allowing you to understand. In those moments, do your best to faithfully reflect the heart of Christ, and then release the rest to Him.

Making Space for God

Although this lesson focuses on discernment in your work as a healthcare leader, it also speaks to your relationship with God more broadly. By creating moments of stillness, you can seek God's wisdom in every area of your life. It is only when we quiet our minds and turn them toward God that we begin to sense His presence, hear His voice, and experience His peace.

Once we establish this pattern in our own lives, we can begin to look for ways to reflect it in the organizational culture we are shaping. In faith-based organizations, this can be grounded in our relationship with God through Jesus Christ. Yet we can also cultivate spaces for stillness and reflection within secular healthcare organizations.

Ways to Cultivate Space for Stillness and Discernment in Your Organization

- Create quiet rooms or reflection spaces where staff can pause, breathe, and reset, even for a minute.
- Begin key meetings with a moment of silence for reflection, grounding, or prayer (in faith-based settings).
- Encourage brief "pause practices" before major decisions, difficult conversations, or crisis situations.
- Model unhurried leadership by showing that thoughtful reflection is valued over rushed reaction.
- Provide optional spiritual resources, such as Scripture reflections, devotionals, or prayer support, for those who want them.
- Invite chaplains or spiritual care leaders to offer guidance, support, and presence during times of organizational stress.
- Normalize taking short breaks to step outside, breathe deeply, or reset when overwhelmed.
- Offer retreats or reflection days that allow teams to step back from daily pressures and reconnect with purpose.
- Cultivate psychologically safe teams where speaking openly, asking questions, and seeking wisdom are valued.
- Protect margins in schedules by limiting unnecessary meetings, allowing space for thoughtful preparation and decision-making.

By following these practices and embracing discernment in your decision-making, you will be doing something rare in today's healthcare environment. Many believe there is no time for intentional reflection. In some contexts, it may even seem outdated. But make no mistake: this is one of the most powerful practices you can adopt.

When you take time to slow down and seek God, you invite Him into every decision. When you pause, He is there. When you communicate decisions and move forward, He remains present. You are not alone. You do not have to rely solely on your own strength.

Over time, this discipline shapes how you relate to others, how you navigate complexity, and how you lead through uncertainty. Just as importantly, it draws you closer to God, deepening your trust in Him day by day.

Action Step 1: Pause before Acting

When faced with an important decision, take a brief moment to reflect rather than reacting immediately. Even a short pause allows space for clarity, counsel, and prayer.

Action Step 2: Seek God's Wisdom Daily

Make a habit of asking for guidance through Scripture, prayer, and reflection, even in small decisions. Over time, this builds discernment and strengthens your leadership.

Action Step 3: Gather Trusted Counsel

Consult team members, mentors, or spiritual advisors before making significant decisions. Listen carefully to insights and perspectives you may not have considered.

Action Step 4: Create Sacred Spaces for Reflection

Establish moments or environments, either personally or within your organization, for stillness, prayer, or meditation. Encourage staff to use these spaces to reset and seek guidance.

Reflection and Journal Prompts

1. Think about a recent decision you made quickly. How might pausing, seeking counsel, or bringing it to God have changed the outcome or your perspective?
2. How do you currently invite God into your decision-making process? What small, consistent practices could you add to deepen your discernment?
3. Who are the trusted individuals you can turn to for guidance in your leadership? How might you intentionally involve them in future decisions?
4. What changes could you make in your daily routine or organizational culture to allow more moments of reflection, stillness, and prayer? How would these moments impact your leadership and decision-making?

Lesson 37

Stand with Conviction

For Christians, conviction is a deep, unwavering certainty about core beliefs that call us to reflect Christ's character. It is a firmness of belief that shapes our decisions and inspires faithful action, even when the path forward is unclear or unpopular. It is not just about following Christ's teachings. It is about embodying His heart.

Why Conviction Matters

- **Clarity of Purpose**. It brings moral clarity in complex healthcare environments where the right decision is not always obvious.
- **Moral Leadership**. It empowers leaders to do what is right, even when that choice is unpopular, inconvenient, or contrary to prevailing expectations.
- **Consistency**. People follow leaders who are grounded and steady. Conviction builds that consistency and earns long-term trust.
- **Scriptural Foundation**. Rooted in Scripture, conviction is modeled by many individuals, including Paul, and ultimately by Christ Himself, who demonstrated unwavering faith at great personal cost.

Yet conviction is not rigidity. It is grounded in openness, humility, and a willingness to listen. Conviction holds firm to what matters most while remaining receptive to wisdom and collaboration.

 DOI: 10.4324/9781003769781-41

Conviction in Scripture: The Example of Daniel

One of the clearest biblical examples of conviction under pressure is Daniel. A young Jewish exile in Babylon, Daniel served in the king's court, surrounded by a culture that did not share his faith or values. He faced constant pressure to compromise, such as eating food sacrificed to idols, worshiping the king, or concealing his faith to protect his position.

But Daniel remained rooted in his identity as God's servant. When a royal decree outlawed prayer to anyone but the king, Daniel didn't rebel loudly. He simply kept praying, just as he always had. His faithfulness led to the lions' den, but also to God's deliverance and a powerful witness to the king.

Christian healthcare leaders may not face lions, but they do face subtle, systemic pressures. These include staying quiet on ethical concerns, compromising values for efficiency, or prioritizing financial goals over patient-centered care. Daniel's example reminds us that conviction often looks like quiet, consistent faithfulness, even when personal risk is real.

What Conviction Looks Like Today

What does conviction look like in modern healthcare?

- A nurse manager advocating for safe staffing levels, even when it's unpopular with administration.
- A physician refusing to upcode diagnoses to improve reimbursement.
- A CEO prioritizing quality of care over profit margins, even at the risk of disappointing investors or board members.

These are not dramatic moments. They are quiet, steady choices made from spiritual depth. That is what Christlike conviction looks like in healthcare.

Living with Conviction

Conviction does not mean having all the answers. It means knowing what anchors you when the path is unclear. As a healthcare leader, you will face tough questions:

- Do I speak up when patient safety is compromised?
- Do I resist pressure to prioritize profit over people?
- Do I lead with compassion when patients become data points?

Sometimes, there will be no easy answers. You will want to prioritize patient safety, put people first, lead with compassion, and ensure financial health all at once. But resources are limited. Tough choices often come quietly, in staff meetings, budget discussions, and small moments when no one is watching. In these moments, pause and reflect:

- What values are non-negotiable for you as a Christian leader?
- What are your core beliefs?
- What would Jesus do in this situation?

Remember that conviction is Christ's presence within you, guiding your choices and giving you courage to lead with integrity. It does not remove every difficult decision, but it grounds you in what truly matters. When the path is unclear and pressure mounts, conviction keeps your heart aligned with Christ's. You may not have all the answers, but you will never walk alone. Lead faithfully, knowing that your commitment honors God and makes a lasting difference in the lives you serve.

Action Step 1: Name Your Non-Negotiables

Identify three core values that reflect your faith and leadership. Write them down, and revisit them regularly, especially when facing difficult decisions.

Action Step 2: Pause Before Pressure

In moments of stress or complexity, take a brief pause to pray, reflect, or ask: *What would Jesus do here?* Let conviction, not urgency, guide your next step.

Action Step 3: Practice Quiet Integrity

Choose one small but meaningful way to act with quiet faithfulness this week, especially when no one is watching. Integrity is built in ordinary moments.

Action Step 4: Find Accountability

Share your commitment to lead with conviction with a trusted peer or mentor. Invite them to ask how you're doing and support you in staying grounded.

Journal and Reflection Prompts

1. When have I felt pressure to compromise my values as a leader? Describe the situation. What did you choose, and what guided that decision? What would you do the same or differently next time?
2. What are the core beliefs that anchor my leadership? List them. Then reflect: How clearly are these convictions showing up in my everyday decisions and interactions?
3. Who is a leader I admire for their conviction? What specific qualities or actions reflect their integrity? How might their example inspire your own leadership path?
4. Where in my leadership do I need courage right now? What situation or decision is challenging your convictions? Ask God to show you the next faithful step and write a prayer for strength and clarity.

Lesson 38

Practice Patience

Patience is one of the hardest disciplines to master, yet it touches every part of our lives. It shapes how we react, the decisions we make, the words we speak, and how we relate to others. At its core, patience is about learning to trust God's timing and His process. For Christian healthcare leaders, it is far from passive. It is a formative practice that shapes leadership with wisdom, faith, and restraint.

Patience in Our Decisions

This kind of patience runs counter to the pace of modern society and the pressures within healthcare organizations. In an environment where speed is often demanded, it takes courage to slow down. Choosing to pause can easily be labeled as avoidance. Yet this kind of disciplined restraint protects leaders from reactive, fear-based choices. While impatience often feels decisive, it is patience that makes decisions durable.

With that said, patience can be hard. Healthcare often produces a constant state of urgency, driven by staffing shortages, quality metrics, and operational pressures. In this environment, leaders feel pressured to act quickly and may be tempted to offer quick fixes rather than wise, sustainable solutions. But here is an important truth: not every problem requires an immediate answer. In fact, decisions made too quickly may resolve a short-term issue but inadvertently create new problems down the line.

 DOI: 10.4324/9781003769781-42

Patience with Others

Patience is also essential in how we relate to others, including leaders, teams, and frontline staff. It does not mean avoiding difficult decisions, lowering standards, or neglecting accountability. Rather, it recognizes that growth is relational and often slow. In a healthcare environment marked by rapid change, rising responsibilities, and increasing complexity, allowing people time to develop and adapt is critical.

Trusting God's Timing and Process

Another aspect of patience for Christian leaders is learning to trust God and His timing. Sometimes this occurs when a prayer is not immediately or clearly answered. At other times, it involves waiting when doors do not open as expected, or when progress seems stalled. You may feel overlooked, stuck, or pressured in your role. In these moments, patience becomes an act of faith, trusting that God's purposes are at work even when they are not yet visible.

This trust often grows over time as you deepen your personal relationship with God. Through daily prayer, conversation, and time spent in His presence, patience and trust naturally increase. It can be deeply liberating to fully surrender to God, having done all you can and leaving the rest in His hands. As a reminder of the power of patience and endurance, Scripture encourages us:

> Be patient, then, brothers and sisters, until the Lord's coming. See how the farmer waits for the land to yield its valuable crop, patiently waiting for the autumn and spring rains. You too, be patient and stand firm, because the Lord's coming is near.
>
> James 5:7–8 (NIV)

The Cost of Impatience

It is also important to reflect on the cost of impatience. When I was leading senior living communities, I was passionate about transforming institutional care settings into homelike environments rooted in person-centered care. This work was part of a broader, values-based national movement.

Looking back, I did not fully understand how some operational changes would impact direct caregivers. I was eager to implement changes quickly to benefit our residents, many of whom did not have much time left to live. My intentions were good, but in my haste, I did not give the concerns of those closest to the work the reflection they deserved.

As a result, unexpected consequences emerged that could have been avoided with a more thoughtful and intentional approach. It also damaged trust in leadership and left people feeling that their perspectives were undervalued. This experience became a pivotal lesson that shaped how I led from that point forward.

Simple Practices for Leaders

The following are simple practices leaders can use in these situations:

- **Pause Before Responding**. Take a moment to reflect before making decisions, especially in high-pressure situations.
- **Seek Multiple Perspectives**. Consult with others, including those closest to the work, before implementing changes to uncover potential consequences.
- **Set Reflection Windows**. Build intentional time into your schedule to think, pray, and discern before acting.
- **Pray and Reflect**. Incorporate daily prayer or meditation to strengthen spiritual patience and perspective.
- **Focus on Relationships**. Invest time in understanding your team's needs, concerns, and growth, remembering that change is relational.
- **Practice the "24-Hour Rule"**. When possible, delay major decisions for a short period to avoid reactive choices.
- **Celebrate Small Wins**. Recognize incremental progress in people and systems to reinforce patience as a positive process.

Cultivating a Culture of Patience

When we practice patience in our own lives, we can gradually weave it into the culture of our organizations. Leaders can encourage open dialogue, invite feedback, and create space for thoughtful decision-making instead of rushing to solutions. They can also recognize and value incremental progress, helping teams understand that meaningful growth takes time.

Other expressions of patience include celebrating reflection, listening actively, and responding thoughtfully. Together, these practices communicate that patience is not a weakness, but a strength. Over time, they foster an environment where staff feel heard, respected, and empowered to do their best work, even amid the pressures of modern healthcare.

In the end, patience is more than a personal virtue. It is a formative leadership practice that shapes how we respond under pressure, make decisions, and relate to others. When cultivated intentionally, patience strengthens organizations, fosters healthier cultures, and deepens our trust in God as we learn to rest in His timing and wisdom.

A Prayer for Patience

Gracious and faithful God,
Teach us patience in every area of our lives.
Give us patience in our decisions,
so we may pause, discern wisely, and act with calm rather than haste.
Give us patience with others,
with those we lead, those we serve, and those who challenge us,
remembering that growth is relational and often slow.
Give us patience in waiting,
when answers are unclear, doors remain closed,
and Your timing does not match our own.
Help us trust that You are at work even when we cannot yet see it.
Form in us a patience shaped by love, humility, and faith,
so that our leadership reflects Your wisdom, grace, and care.
Amen.

Action Step 1: Pause and Reflect Before Acting

Before responding to a challenge or making a decision, take an intentional moment to slow down. Consider the potential consequences and pray for guidance, resisting the urge to act purely from urgency or emotion.

Action Step 2: Listen and Engage with Others

Make space to hear the perspectives of your team, especially those closest to the work. Recognize that people grow at different paces and that relational patience strengthens trust and collaboration.

Action Step 3: Create Deliberate Waiting Spaces

Build reflection and discernment into your schedule. Use tools like the "24-hour rule" or scheduled thinking time to ensure decisions are thoughtful and sustainable, rather than reactive.

Action Step 4: Trust God's Timing in Leadership

Integrate prayer, reflection, and spiritual discernment into your decision-making. Remember that waiting is not inaction. Trusting God allows His wisdom and timing to guide your leadership and your organization.

Reflection and Journal Prompts

1. Reflect on a recent decision where you felt pressured to act quickly. How might taking additional time or seeking more perspectives have changed the outcome?
2. Consider a relationship at work where you've felt frustrated or impatient. How could you practice patience and foster growth in that situation?
3. Identify an area of your leadership or life where you feel stuck or overlooked. How can you surrender this to God and trust His timing, rather than forcing immediate results?
4. Think about a time when impatience led to unintended consequences in your work or leadership. What lessons can you take from that experience to cultivate patience moving forward?

Lesson 39

Navigate Seasons of Loss

Healthcare is often described as demanding, but the feelings of loss that accompany it are less often acknowledged. Leaders grieve the loss of patients. They grieve colleagues lost to burnout or resignation. They grieve when work that once felt like a calling begins to feel hollow, and when meaning is replaced by metrics. Many also grieve a deeper loss, the loss of innocence that comes from seeing healthcare systems fail the people they were meant to protect.

These losses are rarely named. Healthcare culture rewards competence, composure, and forward motion. Leaders are expected to stabilize others and project confidence, even amid profound disappointment. As a result, grief is often deferred or minimized. Yet unnamed loss does not disappear. It shapes how leaders think, decide, relate, and endure.

For Christians, experiencing seasons of loss is not a sign of insufficient faith. It is part of what it means to lead in broken systems and among vulnerable people. This chapter begins by naming these losses honestly, not to dwell in despair, but to create space for truth. Only leaders willing to understand loss are prepared to guide others with wisdom, compassion, and hope.

The Language of Loss

One of the most urgent challenges facing healthcare leaders today is burnout. This is a state of emotional, mental, and physical exhaustion that can leave leaders feeling detached, depleted, and unable to fully

DOI: 10.4324/9781003769781-43

engage with their work. Closely related is moral distress, which arises when leaders know the right course of action but are constrained by policies, resources, or institutional pressures, leaving them frustrated and conflicted.

When leaders are forced to participate in decisions that violate deeply held moral or ethical beliefs, the result can be moral injury. This is a lasting psychological, emotional, or spiritual wounding. Examples include making staffing decisions that compromise patient safety, implementing budget cuts that harm staff well-being, or closing programs that serve vulnerable populations due to financial constraints.

For many leaders, the hardest challenge is forgiving themselves when the best available option still causes harm. Difficult decisions are often replayed long after others have moved on, and moral injury can turn inward as shame. Some wounds are not the result of doing too little, but of doing the best possible with limited and imperfect options.

For leaders, learning to reframe these moments with honesty and self-forgiveness is essential. Without this grace, moral injury hardens into shame and erodes the spirit. With it, leaders can remain anchored in integrity, continue to lead with compassion, and sustain the clarity needed to navigate imperfect systems without losing themselves.

When Leadership Feels Lonely

Loneliness is another form of loss that many healthcare leaders experience. As leadership roles expand, opportunities for genuine peer support narrow. Leaders may remain connected to boards and executive teams yet still feel set apart by the role itself. What is often missed is the closeness of shared work and a sense of belonging. Without those relationships, the weight of other losses can feel heavier and more difficult to bear.

As responsibility increases, permission to grieve often decreases. Leaders feel constant pressure to project calm, certainty, and hope, even while carrying the weight of workforce losses, organizational failures, or decisions set in motion long before they assumed their role. I experienced this personally, feeling a deep sense of responsibility, even for issues outside of my control. It is important to recognize that loneliness is not a leadership flaw. It is a leadership reality. At the same time, unshared grief is unhealthy.

Leaders can acknowledge and address these experiences in constructive ways, including those below.

- **Find trusted peers or mentors**
  Share experiences with colleagues or mentors who understand the unique pressures of leadership.
- **Create structured reflection time**
  Schedule moments for personal reflection, journaling, or prayer to process decisions and emotions.
- **Set boundaries for self-care**
  Protect time for rest, family, and activities that restore energy and perspective.
- **Seek professional support**
  Executive coaches, spiritual advisors, or counselors can provide confidential guidance and insight.
- **Name and acknowledge loss publicly when appropriate**
  Being honest with your team about challenges or organizational setbacks can reduce isolation and build trust.
- **Practice self-forgiveness**
  Recognize that moral injury and difficult decisions are part of leading in complex, constrained systems, and allow yourself grace.

By intentionally addressing loneliness and grief, leaders can preserve their own well-being while sustaining the capacity to lead with integrity, compassion, and clarity.

Navigating Loss without Losing Your Soul

It is important to recognize that unresolved grief can harden leaders. You may have encountered individuals like this, leaders whose emotional detachment, over-reliance on policy, and cynicism disguised as realism are difficult to miss. This hardening is not only harmful to the soul. It also undermines the quality and credibility of leadership.

Loss does not automatically produce wisdom. It must be attended to. When grief is engaged honestly and intentionally, it can deepen compassion, humility, and moral clarity. The goal is not to avoid being wounded by leadership, but to remain fully human within it. We are called to carry loss without allowing it to erode our character, our calling, or our capacity to lead with integrity.

Leading Others Through Loss

In addition to navigating loss personally, one of the most important capacities for healthcare leaders today is guiding others through recurring seasons of loss, burnout, and exhaustion. These challenges often reflect systemic pressures, yet few leaders receive formal training to address them. Leading well in these moments requires sensitivity, honesty, and the ability to model healthy responses to grief. The framework that follows outlines what to avoid, what faithful leadership sounds like, and how to express grief without undermining authority.

What Leaders Should Not Say

Certain phrases, though often well-intentioned, can invalidate grief, increase cynicism, or unintentionally encourage silence. Leaders should avoid the following:

- **"This is just part of the job."**
  Minimizes real emotional and moral burdens.
- **"Other teams have it worse."**
  Encourages comparison and guilt rather than acknowledgment.
- **"Don't let it affect your work."**
  Signals that feelings are inappropriate, fostering shame or suppression.
- **"It's all in God's hands. Just pray."**
  While spiritually true, this can feel dismissive if offered without empathy or practical support.

What Faithful Leadership Sounds Like

Faithful leadership validates experience, offers support, and encourages constructive reflection. Examples include:

- **"I see how hard this is, and it matters that you're feeling this."**
  Acknowledges the reality of stress and loss.

- **"Let's talk about what we can do together to support each other."**
  Encourages shared problem-solving and connection.
- **"It's normal to feel drained. Your work is valuable even when it feels overwhelming."**
  Normalizes emotion while reaffirming purpose.
- **"I'm committed to hearing your concerns and helping where I can."**
  Combines empathy with practical leadership responsibility.

Modeling Grief without Losing Authority

Leaders can demonstrate honesty about loss without undermining confidence or credibility:

- **Share appropriate personal experiences**
  Briefly illustrating your own challenges shows authenticity while maintaining professionalism.
- **Normalize reflection and emotion**
  Encourage team members to acknowledge feelings through structured check-ins or debriefs.
- **Demonstrate resilience while protecting personal well-being**
  Show that grief can coexist with action, decision-making, and steady leadership.
- **Encourage peer and spiritual support**
  Point team members to mentors, colleagues, or chaplains as resources for guidance and processing.
- **Follow through with action**
  Pair acknowledgment of loss with concrete steps to support staff, address systemic challenges, or celebrate successes.

By avoiding dismissive statements, speaking faithfully and empathetically, and modeling healthy engagement with grief, leaders can guide their teams through loss while sustaining both morale and moral clarity. In doing so, they help create a culture where grief is acknowledged, resilience is cultivated, and hope remains possible even amid systemic challenges.

Hope That Is Real

As Christians, one of our most important responsibilities is to share hope with others. Yet Christian hope does not bypass grief. For leaders, this means acknowledging unfinished healing, being honest that recovery takes time, and trusting God's presence even within broken systems. Hope in seasons of loss is not the absence of grief. It is the refusal to let grief have the final word. As Isaiah reminds us:

> But those who hope in the Lord will renew their strength. They will soar on wings like eagles; they will run and not grow weary, they will walk and not be faint.
>
> Isaiah 40:31 (NIV)

Even in the weight of loss, leaders can trust that God's strength will sustain them. Hope is the assurance that grief is not the final chapter, that strength can be renewed, and that perseverance enables us to continue leading with compassion, integrity, and courage.

Action Step 1: Name Your Losses Honestly

Take time to identify the personal and professional losses you are experiencing. Write them down, reflect on them, and resist minimizing their impact.

Action Step 2: Process Grief Intentionally

Engage in practices that allow grief to be worked through: journaling, prayer, meditation, or talking with trusted peers or mentors.

Action Step 3: Model Resilient Leadership

Demonstrate that it is possible to lead with integrity and compassion while carrying difficult decisions. Protect your well-being and encourage your team to do the same.

Action Step 4: Anchor in Hope and Faith

Remind yourself and your team that grief is not the final word. Draw strength from scripture, spiritual practices, and the assurance of God's sustaining presence.

Reflection and Journal Prompts

1. What are the personal and professional losses I have experienced in my leadership journey? How have they shaped the way I lead and relate to others?
2. Recall a decision where you acted under constraint and it caused harm despite your best intentions. What feelings arise when you revisit it, and how might you offer yourself grace?
3. How do I respond to my own grief and the grief of my team? Are there ways I defer, minimize, or spiritualize loss that may hinder healthy processing?
4. In what ways can I lean on God's presence, scripture, or spiritual practices to sustain hope and resilience for myself and those I lead? How can I model this for others?

Lesson 40

Persevere with Hope

One of the most important abilities for healthcare leaders is perseverance. Yet this is often easier said than done. Leadership roles are intensely demanding, and turnover remains alarmingly high across the field. The reality is that chronic stress, heavy workloads, long hours, ethical conflicts, limited resources, stakeholder pressures, personnel challenges, legal demands, and constant scrutiny from surveyors and accreditation agencies can make these roles feel unsustainable. Leaders often find themselves navigating competing interests within systems that are already strained.

Even when they remain in the field, many move from organization to organization, hoping to find a healthier environment. In these conditions, perseverance means more than endurance alone. It means continuing faithfully despite setbacks, trusting God's promises, and resisting the temptation to compromise integrity when the path forward is uncertain or costly.

Perseverance in Scripture

Scripture does not romanticize perseverance. Again and again, God's leaders are shown pressing forward while weary, opposed, and uncertain. Biblical hope is not rooted in favorable conditions, but in the faithfulness of God across time. These stories remind us that perseverance is not the absence of struggle, but the decision to remain faithful within it.

Moses led a people who complained persistently, resisted direction, and repeatedly turned away from God. His leadership was marked by

DOI: 10.4324/9781003769781-44

exhaustion, frustration, and long stretches without affirmation. Yet Moses repeatedly interceded for the very people who tested his resolve. His story reminds us that perseverance often means continuing to lead faithfully even when gratitude is absent and clarity feels elusive.

Nehemiah faced a different kind of resistance. As he worked to rebuild Jerusalem's walls, opposition came through threats, ridicule, and internal division. His perseverance was not blind persistence, but discernment. Nehemiah learned when to press forward despite fear and when to refuse distractions disguised as reasonable or even noble alternatives. His leadership shows that endurance requires wisdom as much as courage.

Paul's perseverance was deeply personal and costly. He openly named his suffering, including imprisonment, hardship, rejection, and physical weakness. Yet he refused to abandon his calling. Rather than denying his limitations, Paul acknowledged them and found his strength in God's sustaining grace. His life testifies that Christian perseverance does not depend on resilience alone, but on reliance. Together, these stories remind us that perseverance in leadership is rarely dramatic or immediate. More often, it is the quiet, faithful decision to remain present, discerning, and obedient in the work God has entrusted to us.

Perseverance as a Season

It is often helpful to think about perseverance in terms of seasons of life. When circumstances are difficult, it is easy to catastrophize and assume that things will always remain this way. But that is rarely true, and recognizing this can be encouraging.

Viewing our work as faithfulness within a particular season often makes the burden feel more manageable. We can say, "I will do the best I can in this position, in this season," rather than feeling trapped by an indefinite future. This alone can be deeply liberating.

At times, it may also be helpful to have a sense of how long a season might last before moving into a different role, organization, or sector. That timeframe might be shaped by a specific goal you have set for your organization, a difficult period you are helping them navigate, or a longer-term vocational plan. It may also be informed by an honest understanding of your personal capacity for the stress of the position.

By thinking of perseverance as seasonal, leaders can remain faithful in their work while maintaining perspective and protecting their well-being.

It reminds us that faithfulness does not require ignoring limits or denying fatigue. Every season has a purpose, and God's timing often unfolds in ways we cannot yet see.

The Importance of Personal Health and Well-Being

While it is important for leaders to find ways to persevere, it is equally important to do so in ways that protect personal health and well-being. I often remind leaders that nothing is worth sacrificing your physical, mental, or spiritual health. Even if you do so temporarily, you will not remain effective as a leader, and the consequences can extend to both you and your family.

This erosion of well-being is often slow and insidious. You may not recognize right away that burnout is creeping in, that your mental health is suffering, or that your physical health is declining. Yet mind, body, and spirit are deeply interconnected, and over time the signs begin to emerge. These may include:

- Chronic fatigue that does not improve with rest
- Emotional numbness, irritability, or increased reactivity
- Persistent feelings of anxiety, sadness, or low mood
- Difficulty concentrating, making decisions, or finding motivation
- Changes in sleep patterns, appetite, or physical health
- Frequent headaches, muscle tension, or unexplained aches and pains
- Recurrent illnesses or a weakened immune response
- Loss of joy or meaning in work that once felt purposeful
- Withdrawal from relationships, community, or spiritual practices
- A persistent sense of pressure to keep going despite diminishing capacity

When leaders begin to notice these signs, it can be tempting to push through and minimize their significance. But doing so is a mistake and often accelerates harm. Instead, consider how to persevere while actively protecting your health. Examples include:

- Recognizing early warning signs of burnout, anxiety, depression, and physical strain before they escalate

- Setting and protecting boundaries around work hours, responsibilities, and availability
- Prioritizing physical health through regular exercise, sleep, proper nutrition, and appropriate medical care
- Practicing daily stress management through meditation, mindfulness, or other grounding techniques
- Delegating and seeking support from teams, mentors, or peers to reduce isolation and overwhelm
- Maintaining emotional and spiritual well-being through relationships, reflection, or spiritual practices
- Evaluating and addressing root causes of stress in your role or environment, recognizing that temporary coping strategies are insufficient without systemic change

Finding a Balance

In the end, there must be a balance between perseverance and personal health. If you are able to persevere with appropriate coping techniques, that is often ideal. But if your health continues to deteriorate, it may be a sign that something needs to change. Some positions and circumstances are no-win situations where no amount of coping will eliminate the pressure, strain, or harm. Other situations can be managed more effectively, depending on the individual and the circumstances.

Here is one thing I do know: while you may be called to the field of healthcare, God loves you and does not want you to be unwell. He would not want you to remain in a situation that is harmful to your body, mind, or spirit. You have been given unique gifts and crafted in a special way. No one else is like you. Some positions and settings will be a good fit for your gifts, and others will not. Part of our journey as Christian healthcare leaders is discerning where we are meant to serve and how our gifts can be used most effectively.

With this in mind, do your best to persevere and walk in faith. When changes are necessary, trust that discernment is part of faithfulness, not a failure of it. In all things, hold fast to this promise as you seek wisdom and direction:

> "For I know the plans I have for you," declares the Lord, "plans to prosper you and not to harm you, plans to give you hope and a future."
>
> Jeremiah 29:11 (NIV)

May this assurance guide your decisions and encourage your heart. It reminds us that caring for ourselves is not separate from serving others, but essential to it. Faithful leadership includes stewardship of the life and health God has entrusted to us.

Action Step 1: Set Healthy Boundaries

Define clear limits around work hours, responsibilities, and availability. Protecting your time and energy ensures you can serve effectively without sacrificing your health.

Action Step 2: Monitor Your Well-Being

Regularly check in with yourself, physically, emotionally, and spiritually. Notice early signs of stress, burnout, or strain, and take proactive steps to address them before they escalate.

Action Step 3: Seek Support and Delegate

Build a network of mentors, peers, and team members to share responsibilities, gain perspective, and reduce isolation. Asking for help is a strength, not a weakness.

Action Step 4: Align Work with Calling

Continually evaluate whether your role and environment allow your gifts to flourish. When necessary, make changes to preserve your health, integrity, and ability to serve faithfully.

Reflection and Journal Prompts

1. What season of leadership am I in right now? Am I in a time of growth, challenge, or transition? How does this perspective affect how I approach my responsibilities?

2. Which signs of physical, mental, or spiritual strain do I notice in myself? How have I responded to these signs so far, and what changes might I consider?
3. Who or what helps me persevere faithfully? Are there mentors, colleagues, spiritual practices, or coping strategies I could lean on more intentionally?
4. How well does my current role align with my unique gifts and sense of calling? Are there adjustments I need to make, small or large, to serve faithfully while protecting my health?

V

LEGACY AND ETERNAL IMPACT

Lesson 41

Empower Others

In healthcare, empowerment means giving others the authority, confidence, resources, and support they need to be successful in their work. For Christian healthcare leaders, it also means helping others to grow and thrive with the gifts, talents, and callings God has entrusted to them. At the same time, empowerment requires trusting God to work through others and loosening our own grip on control.

Delegation vs. Empowerment

The reality of healthcare often leaves little room for true development, growth, or support. Instead, it is more common to delegate rather than empower others. Many healthcare leaders are overwhelmed with responsibilities due to role consolidation and increasing administrative demands. As a result, they may delegate tasks quickly and reactively. While this may provide temporary relief, it can be disempowering for those impacted by the additional workload.

Consider the following distinctions. Delegation focuses primarily on tasks, while empowerment focuses on people. Delegation retains control, with leaders directing how work should be done. Empowerment shares ownership, allowing others to exercise judgment and grow in responsibility. Delegation may address short-term workload issues, but empowerment builds long-term capacity within individuals and teams.

Consider a department manager who assigns additional responsibilities to a supervisor without sufficient authority, training, or support. The task

DOI: 10.4324/9781003769781-46

has been delegated, but the supervisor remains constrained and exposed to risk. Or consider a hospital director who asks a service line leader to lead an initiative but continues to override decisions at every turn. In both cases, work has been transferred, but leadership has not been developed.

When delegation is driven by exhaustion rather than intention, it can strain trust and damage relationships. Those receiving the work are often already overwhelmed. Instead of feeling valued and developed, they may feel used or set up to fail. Over time, this erodes morale and weakens teams rather than strengthening them. True empowerment requires a deliberate approach. It involves pacing responsibility, providing clarity and support, and allowing others to lead even when it feels uncomfortable.

Empowerment as Spiritual Formation

For Christian leaders, it can be helpful to think about leadership development as a form of spiritual formation. From this perspective, empowerment is not only about outcomes or performance, but about who people are becoming through their work. It involves patience with growth and mistakes, recognizing that learning often happens slowly and unevenly. Empowerment allows others to struggle without immediate rescue, while still providing guidance and support when needed.

Formation-oriented empowerment also requires creating environments of psychological safety. People must know they can speak honestly, ask questions, and take responsible risks without fear of humiliation or retaliation. This kind of safety strengthens accountability by allowing leaders to address mistakes openly and constructively.

Above all, empowerment as formation depends on what leaders model. Humility, teachability, and accountability shape culture far more than policies or training programs. When leaders acknowledge their own limits, invite feedback, and take responsibility for their decisions, they create space for others to do the same.

Practicing this kind of empowerment takes time, which is challenging in the current healthcare environment. Assigning tasks is far easier than investing in the slower work of developing leaders. Yet for Christian healthcare leaders, this work is part of the calling. It is closely tied to faithfulness and to the long-term sustainability of both leaders and organizations.

Empowerment in Faith-Based and Secular Settings

Christian healthcare leaders often serve in diverse environments that include both faith-based and secular organizations. While language and context may differ, the heart of empowerment remains the same. In faith-based settings, leaders can speak openly about Christ and Scripture, while in secular settings, empowerment can be expressed through fairness, dignity, trust, and genuine investment in people. In both contexts, leaders bear witness not only through words, but through how they develop others, share responsibility, and lead with integrity.

Regardless of the setting, the greatest risk of empowering others lies in how it is experienced. In environments marked by chronic understaffing, constant change, and mounting demands, empowerment can easily be perceived as the transfer of stress rather than the sharing of leadership. When responsibilities are handed off without clarity, support, or attention to capacity, those receiving them may feel overwhelmed rather than trusted. Instead of fostering growth, empowerment can unintentionally breed resentment and fatigue.

Leaders must therefore practice empowerment with wisdom, restraint, and care. It is not about shifting burdens downward, but about cultivating leadership upward. With this in mind, the following practices offer practical ways Christian healthcare leaders can empower others faithfully and sustainably.

Practices of Empowering Leadership

- **Assess capacity before assigning responsibility**
  Take time to understand current workloads, emotional strain, and competing priorities. Empowerment should stretch people, not break them.
- **Match responsibility with authority and support**
  Do not ask people to carry outcomes they lack the authority or resources to influence. Clear decision rights, access to information, and visible leader support are essential.
- **Pace empowerment over time**
  Growth happens incrementally. Introduce new responsibilities gradually, allowing space for learning, adjustment, and feedback.

- **Clarify expectations and define success together**
  Co-create goals, timelines, and measures of success to make empowerment collaborative rather than imposed.
- **Stay present without taking over**
  Regular check-ins, coaching, and availability communicate trust without micromanaging.
- **Encourage learning from mistakes**
  Create space to reflect on what worked and what did not without blame, especially in healthcare where fear of error can stifle growth.
- **Affirm growth and effort**
  Acknowledge effort, judgment, and progress, even when outcomes are imperfect. This reinforces development rather than performance alone.
- **Reflect regularly on empowerment**
  Ask whether responsibilities are being shared to develop others or simply to relieve pressure. This reflection keeps empowerment aligned with faithfulness rather than survival.

Empowering Others Faithfully

As I reflect on my own leadership journey, I see moments when I empowered others faithfully and moments when I delegated work simply to survive. You may recognize the same pattern in your own leadership. This kind of reflection matters, especially for those who desire to lead in a more Christlike way.

Regardless of the past, moving forward we can be intentional about what empowerment truly means. For Christian healthcare leaders, clarity matters. When empowerment is grounded in our identity as followers of Christ, it can guide our decisions even in demanding environments. At its best, empowerment creates space for growth. It helps others recognize their gifts, develop their strengths, and step more fully into their calling. When this happens, leaders are sustained, teams are strengthened, and organizations are better able to serve.

Action Step 1: Evaluate Opportunities for Growth

Identify tasks or projects that can help team members develop new skills or take on leadership responsibility.

Action Step 2: Match Responsibility with Support

Ensure each person has the authority, resources, and guidance they need to succeed, not just the workload.

Action Step 3: Pace and Monitor Empowerment

Introduce new responsibilities gradually, check in regularly, and adjust as needed to prevent overwhelm.

Action Step 4: Reflect on Your Leadership Motives

Ask yourself whether you are sharing responsibilities to develop others or simply to relieve your own pressure, and adjust accordingly.

Reflection and Journal Prompts

1. Reflect on recent instances where you delegated tasks. Did you empower others to grow, or were you primarily relieving your own workload?
2. Consider areas where you hold tightly to control. What fears or assumptions underlie this, and how might you trust God to work through others in these areas?
3. Think about team members you lead. Where could you intentionally create space for them to take on new responsibilities or develop leadership skills?
4. How does your behavior create an environment that encourages others to lead faithfully and grow in their potential?

Lesson 42

Grow Leaders of Character

One hallmark of effective leadership is the ability to grow other leaders. For Christian healthcare leaders, it begins with modeling integrity and helping others align their actions with biblically grounded values. This remains true whether one serves in secular or faith-based organizations.

That said, the approach will differ depending on the organization in which you serve. In faith-based organizations, there is often an intentional focus on spiritual formation. Leaders may emphasize aligning decisions and behaviors with Scripture, and prayer can play a role in both personal and professional growth.

In secular organizations, there may be greater emphasis on shared human values. Yet integrity and principled leadership matter here as well. In these environments, Christian healthcare leaders can develop others by living out their faith, demonstrating ethical leadership, and modeling consistency through daily decisions and professional relationships.

This kind of formation is often lacking in academic and professional settings. Education and training frequently emphasize technical skills, knowledge, and performance metrics while offering little guidance on moral, spiritual, or character development. As a result, emerging leaders may be technically competent but underprepared to navigate ethical challenges or exercise sound judgment.

To address this gap deliberate strategies are needed to cultivate integrity and principled behavior in emerging leaders. By focusing not only on performance but also on moral and spiritual formation, leaders can shape others to act with humility, ethical clarity, and discernment. The following practices offer concrete ways to grow leaders of character.

DOI: 10.4324/9781003769781-47

Practical Steps to Grow Leaders of Character

- **Model integrity in daily actions**
  Demonstrate honesty, ethical decision-making, and consistency between words and deeds, showing others what principled leadership looks like in practice.
- **Invest in mentoring and coaching**
  Provide guidance, feedback, and encouragement to help others develop both professionally and morally.
- **Encourage reflection and accountability**
  Create opportunities for leaders to evaluate their decisions, consider their values, and take responsibility for their actions.
- **Cultivate humility and service**
  Emphasize servant leadership, encouraging emerging leaders to prioritize the growth and well-being of their teams.
- **Support spiritual and moral growth**
  In faith-based settings, integrate prayer, Scripture, and discussion of ethical dilemmas to reinforce character formation.
- **Provide opportunities for ethical decision-making**
  Give leaders scenarios where they must navigate complex situations while upholding integrity and godly values.
- **Recognize and reinforce character-based behavior**
  Acknowledge and celebrate actions that reflect honesty, compassion, self-control, and humility, reinforcing these as key leadership qualities.

Creating a Culture of Character

In addition to developing individuals, a leader's responsibility also extends to shaping the broader culture of the organization. It is about creating an environment where ethical behavior, trust, and mutual respect are expected, nurtured, and reinforced. By fostering this kind of culture, leaders create a microcosm of hope, especially when broader leadership may seem disconnected from humanity. In this environment, team members are encouraged to act ethically, support one another, and prioritize shared values over short-term efficiency or immediate results.

Practical Steps to Create a Culture of Character

- **Model ethical behavior**
  Demonstrate consistency in decision-making and interactions, signaling that character matters more than convenience or shortcuts.
- **Communicate values and expectations**
  Clearly articulate the organization's commitment to honesty, compassion, humility, and self-control, integrating these values into policies, evaluations, and daily practices.
- **Celebrate character-driven actions**
  Recognize and reward behaviors that exemplify integrity, collaboration, and ethical leadership, reinforcing these values throughout the team.
- **Encourage dialogue and accountability**
  Promote an environment where team members feel safe raising concerns, asking questions, and holding each other accountable.
- **Provide ongoing education and reflection**
  Offer workshops, discussions, or mentoring on ethical decision-making, moral dilemmas, and the integration of faith and values in professional life.
- **Foster servant leadership**
  Encourage leaders at all levels to serve their teams, putting others' growth and well-being at the center of organizational priorities.

Multiplying Leaders of Character

The development of character follows a clear progression. It begins within ourselves by cultivating integrity, humility, and self-control in our daily actions and decisions. Only then can we mentor and grow other leaders who embrace these principles. As they mature, they influence their teams, shaping an environment where character is embedded throughout the organization.

In this way, principled leadership multiplies outward, creating a culture grounded in ethical behavior, trust, and hope. As Philippians 2:3–4 (NIV) reminds us: *"Do nothing out of selfish ambition or vain conceit. Rather, in humility value others above yourselves, not looking to your own interests but each of you to the interests of the others."*

Action Step 1: Model Integrity Daily

Commit to consistent honesty, ethical decision-making, and transparency in all interactions to demonstrate principled leadership.

Action Step 2: Mentor and Invest in Others

Meet regularly with emerging leaders to provide guidance, feedback, and encouragement for both professional and moral growth.

Action Step 3: Foster Reflection and Accountability

Encourage leaders and team members to regularly reflect on decisions, evaluate alignment with values, and take responsibility for actions.

Action Step 4: Embed Character into Organizational Practices

Integrate values-based expectations into policies, performance evaluations, team rituals, and recognition systems to reinforce ethical behavior and servant leadership.

Reflection and Journal Prompts

1. Reflect on a recent decision or interaction: Did it align with your values and the principles of character you want to model? What would you do differently next time?
2. Who in your team or organization are you actively investing in as a future leader? How can you better support their growth in both skills and character?
3. Identify a situation where you faced an ethical challenge or moral dilemma. How did you respond, and what did you learn about your own character?
4. Consider the culture of your team or organization. What specific actions can you take this week to reinforce integrity, humility, and ethical behavior in your environment?

Lesson 43

Build Genuine Relationships

Great leaders do more than assemble teams. They cultivate genuine, lasting relationships. This extends across the organization, from board members and senior leaders to mid-level managers and frontline staff. Such leaders value every person as an individual, not merely a role or function. They take intentional time to listen, learn, and demonstrate authentic care. In doing so, they foster trust, strengthen collaboration, and model Christlike leadership in both word and deed. The following characteristics illustrate genuine leadership relationships in practice.

Characteristics of Genuine Leadership Relationships

- **Respect for Every Person**
  Genuine leaders treat every individual with dignity, regardless of role, title, or status. They recognize that respect is not earned through position but shown through consistent words and actions. This creates an environment where people feel seen, valued, and safe to contribute.
- **Authentic Care and Empathy**
  Genuine relationships are marked by sincere concern for others as whole people. Effective leaders take time to understand personal challenges, aspirations, and perspectives. They listen with empathy and respond with compassion, reflecting Christ's call to love others selflessly.
- **Consistency and Trustworthiness**
  Trust grows when leaders are consistent in their behavior, decisions, and values. Genuine leaders follow through on commitments,

DOI: 10.4324/9781003769781-48

communicate honestly, and act with integrity even when it is inconvenient. Over time, this consistency builds deep and lasting trust.

- **Humility and Approachability**
  Leaders who build genuine relationships do not place themselves above others. They remain approachable, open to feedback, and willing to admit mistakes. Humility invites dialogue and strengthens connection across all levels of the organization.
- **Presence and Attentiveness**
  Genuine leaders are fully present in their interactions. They give others their time and attention without distraction, recognizing that presence itself communicates value. Small, consistent moments of attentiveness often matter more than grand gestures.
- **Fairness and Equity**
  Authentic leaders treat people fairly and avoid favoritism. They apply standards consistently and advocate for those who may not have a voice. This reinforces trust and demonstrates respect for the entire community.
- **Commitment to Mutual Growth**
  Genuine relationships are dynamic, not static. Effective leaders encourage development, provide constructive feedback, and celebrate growth in others. They see relationships as opportunities for mutual learning and shared progress.

By embracing these characteristics, leaders cultivate relationships that are authentic, transformative, and reflective of Christlike leadership.

The Impact of Culture on Relationships

In addition to forming genuine relationships, leaders must evaluate how policies, processes, and systems shape those relationships across the organization. Even when senior leaders make intentional efforts to connect authentically, the broader culture can limit their impact if organizational policies communicate a different message. Consider a common scenario in healthcare organizations. In some systems, when a leader resigns to join a competitor, they are asked to leave immediately, effectively ending their role on the spot. While such policies are often intended to protect organizational interests, they can carry unintended consequences. They may discourage thoughtful transitions and send a strong message to other staff.

The message can be interpreted as one of caution rather than trust. Staff may come to believe that transparency carries risk and that loyalty is not always reciprocated. Over time, policies like this can erode trust, strain relationships, and undermine the very culture leaders are trying to build.

Departing leaders often carry these experiences forward. Those who feel they were not treated with dignity may be less likely to return as future hires, referral sources, or community partners. In today's era of workforce shortages, such approaches may not only be counterproductive, but can also weaken long-term organizational strength. Leaders who seek to build genuine relationships must therefore examine not only their own behavior but also the policies and systems that shape organizational culture.

Building Relationships as Followers of Christ

For Christian healthcare leaders, this is especially important. Leadership is not just about professionalism or integrity. It is a matter of faith. We must evaluate how we treat others, build relationships, and shape policies through the lens of Jesus' teachings. A helpful guide is to ask questions such as:

- How would Jesus treat this person in this moment?
- What kind of relationship would Jesus build with this individual?
- How would Jesus view this policy?

For instance, would Jesus fire someone for accepting another position? If not, neither should we. Leadership grounded in Christ's example prioritizes dignity, respect, and long-term relationships above short-term convenience or fear.

Many moments won't be this dramatic, but they may be just as important for the person we encounter. We never know what someone is going through, how they may be hurting, or the challenges they face. By forming genuine relationships, we create spaces of trust and support and demonstrate Christlike compassion. This leaves a lasting legacy of care, respect, and encouragement that strengthens both people and the organization.

Action Step 1: Invest Time Intentionally

Schedule regular one-on-one conversations with team members, peers, and external stakeholders. Use these moments to listen deeply, ask meaningful questions, and show genuine interest in each person's experiences, goals, and challenges.

Action Step 2: Model Respect and Fairness

Treat every individual with dignity, regardless of title or role. Ensure that policies, decisions, and everyday actions reflect equity, transparency, and consistency. Remember that how you act sets the tone for the broader organizational culture.

Action Step 3: Practice Presence and Attentive Listening

Be fully present during interactions. Avoid distractions, give your full attention, and respond thoughtfully. Small gestures of attentiveness such as acknowledging achievements, following up on concerns, or checking in on well-being, have a lasting impact.

Action Step 4: Lead with Faith and Integrity

Use Jesus' example as a guide in decision-making, conflict resolution, and policy development. Regularly ask: *How would Christ treat this individual? What kind of relationship would He build? How would He view this choice or policy?* Let faith shape not only your actions but the culture you help create.

Reflection and Journal Prompts

1. Think about the relationships you currently have with your team, peers, and external stakeholders. Who might need more of your time, attention, or intentional care? How can you strengthen these connections this week?
2. Reflect on your recent interactions and decisions. Have your words, actions, or policies consistently conveyed respect and fairness to all individuals, regardless of their position? Where might you improve?
3. Consider your ability to be fully present with others. Are there moments when distractions interfere with attentive listening?

How can you cultivate greater presence in your daily interactions?

4. Reflect on how your faith shapes the relationships you build. In difficult situations, how can you ask yourself, "What would Jesus do?" to guide your words, actions, and decisions? Where do you see opportunities to model Christlike care more consistently?

Lesson 44

Leave No One Behind

Leadership is not defined by results alone. It is measured by how we care for people. For Christian healthcare leaders, this means ensuring that every team member feels seen, valued, and supported. Leaving no one behind requires attentiveness to those who may struggle, feel overlooked, or lack confidence, and a willingness to create meaningful opportunities for them to contribute and grow. It calls us to walk alongside each person, offering guidance, encouragement, and the resources needed to succeed.

When leaders act in this way, they build trust, foster loyalty, and shape a culture where people can truly thrive. Intentional investment in individuals multiplies a leader's influence and creates a lasting legacy of care and inclusion. Leaving no one behind is not simply a leadership strategy. It is a commitment to honoring the inherent worth of every person and refusing to sacrifice people in the pursuit of organizational goals. This commitment reflects God's calling for how we are to treat one another. As the apostle Paul reminds us in 1 Thessalonians 5:11 (NIV):

> Therefore encourage one another and build each other up, just as in fact you are doing.

True leadership leaves no one behind by consistently encouraging, uplifting, and strengthening those entrusted to our care.

DOI: 10.4324/9781003769781-49

Recognizing Those at Risk

This approach often runs counter to the culture of modern healthcare organizations, where everything seems to move faster and grow more complex. As demands increase, those who struggle to keep up, manage heavy workloads, or cope with sustained stress can begin to feel overlooked or expendable. Yet just as Jesus sees each individual as a sacred child of God and a person of infinite worth, so must we.

The field of healthcare is approaching a breaking point. Physical, psychological, and spiritual demands frequently exceed what we are designed to carry in a healthy, sustainable way. When individuals eventually falter or feel compelled to step away, they may come to believe their worth is measured solely by their ability to endure unrealistic expectations. Over time, this quiet erosion of dignity can give rise to anxiety, depression, and profound spiritual harm. Yet in Christ, no one is forgotten. As He promises in John 10:28–29 (NIV):

> I give them eternal life, and they shall never perish; no one will snatch them out of my hand. My Father, who has given them to me, is greater than all; no one can snatch them out of my Father's hand.

Every person holds infinite value and remains secure in His care, regardless of the pressures, struggles, or failures they may face.

Leading with Compassion

As leaders, we can model this care ourselves. It is countercultural to slow down to help a team member when they are struggling, to listen deeply and intentionally, to admit when we have asked too much, and to offer genuine support. Yet this is precisely what it means to lead as a Christian healthcare leader.

This is especially important when people come to you in moments of crisis or vulnerability. These moments should not be seen as individual weakness, but as signals that change is needed, both for the person and the system. High turnover, from frontline staff to CEOs, is another warning sign. Yet these warning signals are often ignored, as it may seem easier to rotate new people in and out than to address broken systems. Now more than ever, leaders should prioritize ways to ensure no one is left behind.

Practical Ways to Ensure No One Is Left Behind

- **Intentionally Notice the Quiet and Struggling**
  Pay attention to those who are withdrawing, underperforming, or unusually silent. Those most at risk of being forgotten are often the quietest or least visible.
- **Create Safe Spaces for Honest Conversation**
  Invite openness without fear of judgment or punishment. When people feel safe to share concerns, exhaustion, or doubt, they are far less likely to suffer in silence.
- **Check In Before Crisis Emerges**
  Check in proactively, before performance fails or a crisis emerges. Regular communication demonstrates care and allows leaders to provide support early.
- **Adjust Expectations When Demands Become Unhealthy**
  When workloads or systems become unsustainable, acknowledge it and make changes. Protecting people is more important than preserving broken processes.
- **Provide Support, Not Just Accountability**
  Pair accountability with coaching, resources, and encouragement. Growth happens when people are supported, not shamed.
- **Advocate for People within the System**
  Use your influence to speak up for those who are overburdened, overlooked, or marginalized. Leadership means standing in the gap for those who cannot advocate for themselves.
- **Remind People of Their Worth Beyond Productivity**
  Reinforce that value is not determined by output, endurance, or performance. People matter because they are people, created in the image of God.

What Being Forgotten Looks Like

Today, many leaders are hired with minimal training, overloaded with responsibilities, and expected to sink or swim on their own. When someone in this position approaches a supervisor in crisis and receives a cold or dismissive response, the sense of being forgotten can deepen. I have experienced both sides of this over the course of my career. As a senior leader, a nursing leader once came to me when she was struggling.

In retrospect, I could have responded with greater compassion and support. At other times, I was the one carrying an unmanageable load and felt that I was not treated with understanding, respect, or dignity.

These experiences have strengthened my desire to become a better leader. Perhaps you can relate. Your past experiences, both positive and negative, can fuel growth as a leader and a follower of Christ. What matters most is not how you begin, but how you respond, learn, and grow along the way.

Taking a Stand

This may be one of the most important lessons in this book. Each of us matters, regardless of our ability to cope with the current expectations of our field. No one deserves to be forgotten, and it is our responsibility as Christians to ensure that no one is left behind.

We must show others that they are not alone. Yes, Christ is with them, but so are we. We have been placed in this moment not only to lead organizations, but to care for the people within them.

Embracing this calling requires making a stand. It means advocating for others, leading counterculturally, offering second chances, validating concerns, and changing systems to prioritize humanity. When leaders choose to stand this way, healthcare organizations become more whole, humane, and faithful to the values they claim to uphold.

At the end of John's Gospel, Jesus gives Peter a simple but demanding charge. Three times He asks, "Do you love me?" and each time He follows with a command: *"Feed my lambs," "Take care of my sheep," and "Feed my sheep"* (John 21:15–17, NIV). Love for Christ is inseparable from care for people. Leadership is measured not only by results or resilience, but by whether we tend to those entrusted to us.

For Christian healthcare leaders, this calling is especially clear. Feeding His sheep involves noticing who is struggling, protecting those who are overwhelmed, and refusing to allow anyone to be overlooked. It also calls us to stand in the gap when systems fail, to choose compassion when efficiency is rewarded, and to care for people with the same faithfulness Christ shows to us.

This is the stand we are called to make. Not just to lead well, but to love well. Not just to manage organizations, but to shepherd people. When we do, leadership becomes more than a role or a title. It becomes an act of faithfulness to the One who entrusted His sheep to our care.

Action Step 1: Notice and Attend to Those at Risk

Pay attention to team members who are struggling, withdrawing, or unusually quiet. Make it a regular practice to check in, offering guidance, encouragement, and support before issues escalate.

Action Step 2: Create Safe Spaces for Honest Conversation

Foster an environment where people can share concerns, doubts, or stress without fear of judgment or retaliation. Listening deeply and empathetically helps people feel valued and reduces isolation.

Action Step 3: Advocate for People within the System

Use your influence to stand up for those who are overburdened, overlooked, or marginalized. Intervene when processes or policies place undue strain on individuals, prioritizing care over efficiency.

Action Step 4: Reinforce Worth Beyond Performance

Remind your team that value is not determined by output, endurance, or results. Celebrate each person as a child of God, encouraging growth, resilience, and faithfulness in a way that honors their inherent dignity.

Reflection and Journal Prompts

1. Reflect on times when you felt overlooked, unsupported, or forgotten in a workplace or leadership role. How did it affect your motivation, trust, and well-being? How might these experiences inform the way you lead others today?

2. Who on your current team might be quietly struggling or withdrawing? List one or two ways you could intentionally notice, check in, and offer support this week.
3. Consider an aspect of your organization's processes, culture, or expectations that might unintentionally overlook or burden people. What is one step you could take to advocate for those affected and create a safer, more supportive environment?
4. How do you currently communicate value and encouragement to your team? Identify at least one concrete action you can take to remind individuals that their worth is not defined solely by results or productivity.

Lesson 45

Impact Beyond Your Walls

As healthcare leaders, it can feel as though there is never enough time or energy to meet the growing demands within our organizations. Yet as Christians, we are also called to look beyond our immediate responsibilities and consider how our leadership can serve the wider community. Faithful leaders engage both their organizations and local communities, bringing hope and support to those in need. When leaders carry their influence beyond their walls, they begin to shape a legacy that reflects God's compassion, multiplies impact, and models servant leadership for others to follow. Jesus reminds us of this responsibility when he says:

> Truly I tell you, whatever you did for one of the least of these brothers and sisters of mine, you did for me.
>
> Matthew 25:40 (NIV)

Discern Where You Are Called to Serve

There are many ways to serve your local community. Some leaders join civic organizations or serve on nonprofit boards, while others partner with schools, faith-based initiatives, or community health efforts. What matters most is that your service is meaningful and aligned with your calling. Through prayer and reflection, you can discern where your strengths are most needed and where God is stirring your heart. When you are intentional about the causes and organizations you support, your service becomes more effective, sustainable, and joyful.

DOI: 10.4324/9781003769781-50

It is also important to emphasize depth over breadth. Choosing one or two organizations to support deeply is often more impactful than participating superficially in many. The reality is that leaders have limited time, and shallow involvement can unintentionally undermine both personal credibility and organizational trust. Community members quickly recognize token participation, and value leaders who engage with genuine commitment.

Navigate Expectations, Boundaries, and Time

While community involvement is important, it is also essential to acknowledge the tension it can create. If you feel this pressure, it is important not to carry unnecessary guilt. A full-time leadership role can already strain holistic health and well-being, particularly when balancing work, family responsibilities, and relationships. When additional expectations are placed on leaders to extend their impact into the wider community, finding true balance can feel even more challenging.

The key is learning to say yes selectively and to say no with integrity. This includes avoiding performative service while intentionally guarding family time and personal health. It is also wise and appropriate to align community involvement with your current season of life and leadership role. For example, leaders with young children may choose forms of service that are more local, time-limited, or family-inclusive, recognizing that capacity changes over time. Faithful leadership honors seasons, and wisdom lies in discerning what faithfulness looks like in each one.

Lead Upstream in Healthcare

Community engagement is not separate from healthcare leadership. It is upstream leadership. In my own career, this truth became clear through a passion for education, growth, and developing others. As a licensed nursing home administrator and later the CEO of a large continuing care retirement community, I invested in the next generation of leaders by serving as a preceptor for administrators in training. This role required additional state licensure and formal partnerships with local universities offering Administrator in Training (AIT) programs. Participants completed a required number of hours across leadership and operational areas, working closely with me and other organizational leaders as they prepared for state and federal licensure examinations.

I served in this capacity for many years and found deep fulfillment in walking alongside emerging leaders. Beyond preparing them for licensure, I intentionally exposed them to the culture change movement within long-term care, an ongoing shift away from institutional models toward person-centered communities. In doing so, I sought to ensure they were not only technically prepared, but also equipped to lead with purpose, compassion, and a clear sense of calling.

In addition to precepting, I supported local communities through adjunct teaching and by offering professional insight to academic and training programs. These opportunities allowed me to contribute practical, real-world experience to the classroom and to help shape curricula that reflected the realities of healthcare leadership. In this way, my engagement extended beyond my own organization to influence the formation of future leaders across the broader continuum of care. Other forms of upstream service include:

- Addressing social determinants of health through community partnerships
- Supporting underserved populations before they enter care
- Collaborating with public health, behavioral health, and social services
- Investing in workforce development in rural or underserved areas
- Viewing community impact as an extension of organizational quality, safety, and mission

Community engagement, then, is not separate from healthcare leadership. It is upstream leadership, shaping the future of care long before individuals ever enter our organizations.

Influence Organizational Culture

Community engagement also influences organizational culture. Teams notice what leaders prioritize, and staff often mirror those priorities. By modeling compassion, humility, and service, you invite others to serve without coercion, creating a ripple effect across the organization.

Integrate Service Sustainably

At the same time, it is essential to integrate service in ways that avoid burnout. While this can be challenging, much of it comes down to mindset. As Christian healthcare leaders, we can view service as an integral part of spiritual formation. As seasons of life and leadership change, we can continually evaluate our commitments through prayer and discernment.

It is equally important to assess our impact honestly and make thoughtful adjustments when needed. The goal is not to do everything, but to be faithful with what God has entrusted to us. It is possible to find a balance that is fulfilling, sustainable, and aligned with your calling. When something no longer feels right, it may be a signal that discernment and change are needed.

Live in Faithful Presence

As we reflect on ways to extend our impact, it is essential to remember that we are more than our current position, title, or role within an organization. We have a unique calling within our families and communities as well. This impact may be quiet and unseen, yet it is no less significant.

God calls us into different spaces across the seasons of our lives, and by listening for His guidance, we are never alone in discerning where to serve. The invitation is to seek balance so that leadership reflects wholeness and intention. Through prayerful discernment, you can embrace a rhythm of service that is sustainable, fulfilling, and aligned with the calling God has placed on your life.

> For we are God's handiwork, created in Christ Jesus to do good works, which God prepared in advance for us to do.
>
> Ephesians 2:10 (NIV)

By living in this truth, your influence will grow quietly but powerfully, touching lives in ways that may never be seen yet carry eternal significance.

Action Step 1: Discern Your Unique Calling

Set aside dedicated time for prayer and reflection to identify where God is calling you to serve in your community. List your strengths, passions, and available time, then match them to potential community opportunities.

Action Step 2: Select Meaningful Engagements

Choose one or two community initiatives where you can make a real impact, rather than spreading yourself too thin. Prioritize depth over breadth, aligning your service with your leadership strengths and current season of life.

Action Step 3: Model Service Through Presence

Be consistently present and actively engaged in your chosen community efforts. Lead by example, demonstrating compassion, humility, and integrity, so that others in your organization are inspired to serve alongside you.

Action Step 4: Evaluate and Adjust Regularly

Periodically assess your commitments, impact, and personal well-being. Use prayerful discernment to make adjustments as needed, ensuring that your service remains sustainable, fulfilling, and aligned with God's calling.

Reflection and Journal Prompts

1. Reflect on the areas of community service where you feel most drawn. What strengths, passions, or experiences does God want you to use in these spaces? How does this align with your current season of life and leadership role?
2. Consider the community commitments you currently have or are considering. Are you spreading yourself too thin, or are you investing deeply in a few areas? How can you prioritize depth and meaningful engagement over simply being visible?
3. Think about the ways your actions as a leader influence your team and organization. How can you model faithful service in your community so that others are inspired to serve without feeling pressured?
4. Reflect on your personal boundaries, energy, and well-being. Are there adjustments you need to make to maintain sustainable service across your work, family, spiritual, and community life? How can prayerful discernment guide you in creating balance?

Lesson 46

Turn Failure into Growth

In healthcare leadership, success is often expected. It may be measured by financial performance, survey results, quality indicators, or a variety of other metrics. Yet even the most capable leaders have only so much control, resources, and influence. As a result, plans will sometimes fall short, and it is how leaders respond in these moments that matters most.

The truth is that setbacks are an inevitable part of leadership. No one is successful all the time. When challenges arise, how you frame the experience is critical. The worst response is to internalize it. Labeling an experience as "failure" can leave a lasting mark, affecting both self-worth and future decisions.

Viewing these moments as setbacks is far healthier. A setback is temporary, not the end of the journey. Framed this way, leaders can respond with reflection, learning, and growth. For Christians, each setback also offers an opportunity to deepen faith, strengthen character, and cultivate empathy and wisdom. Leaders who embrace growth in the midst of setbacks leave a lasting, God-honoring impact on the people and organizations they serve. When leaders extend grace to themselves, they are better able to extend it to others. As Christians, we are reminded:

> For though the righteous fall seven times, they rise again…
>
> Proverbs 24:16 (NIV)

This verse reminds us that falling is normal. It is not a mark of failure, but a natural part of leadership and life. Every leader faces challenges, even

DOI: 10.4324/9781003769781-51

if they are not shared publicly. What matters most is rising again, learning from the experience, and moving forward with faith, humility, and courage.

The Reality of Healthcare Leadership

Healthcare leadership today is marked by constant pressure. Staffing shortages, complex patient needs, regulatory demands, financial constraints, and ethical dilemmas are part of the daily landscape. In this environment, even capable and committed leaders will face situations where outcomes are shaped by factors beyond their control. Effort and expertise do not always lead to success.

Over the course of my career, I encountered many of these challenges, most of which I was able to process in a healthy way. One experience, however, stayed with me. It involved an organizational turnaround effort that ultimately was not successful. Many of the decisions shaping that outcome had been made before my tenure, yet I internalized the result as a personal failure. It left a deep and lasting impression.

With time and perspective, I came to see the situation more clearly. Much of what occurred was outside my direct control and was shaped by market forces, financial realities, and organizational history. At the same time, the experience proved formative. It sharpened my judgment, deepened my humility, and strengthened my empathy for others leading through uncertainty. Those lessons served me well in future roles.

At the time, however, the experience did not feel like a temporary setback. It felt definitive. By framing it as failure rather than growth, I allowed it to influence how I viewed myself and my leadership. Only through honest reflection was I able to reframe the experience for what it truly was: a difficult season that contributed to my growth rather than defining my worth.

This experience reinforced an important truth. In healthcare leadership, setbacks are inevitable. What shapes a leader's legacy is not the absence of failure, but the willingness to learn, grow, and move forward with wisdom and perspective.

Practical Strategies for Turning Setbacks into Growth

It took me many years to fully process that setback and grow from the experience. At the time, I did not yet have the tools or perspective

I do now. Looking back, I can see how much unnecessary weight I carried simply because I did not know how to respond in a healthy and constructive way. With that in mind, the following strategies may help leaders navigate setbacks with greater clarity, resilience, and grace.

- **Reflect honestly, without self-condemnation**
  Growth begins with honest reflection. This requires the discipline to examine what happened, what went well, and what could have been handled differently, without turning the analysis inward in a destructive way. Self-condemnation shuts down learning, while honest reflection opens the door to insight. Effective leaders ask thoughtful questions, seek patterns, and remain curious rather than defensive. Reflection should illuminate lessons, not reinforce shame.
- **Acknowledge what is within your control and what is not**
  Healthcare leaders operate within complex systems where outcomes are influenced by many forces. One of the most important steps after a setback is separating what you could reasonably control from what was beyond your influence. Owning responsibility where it belongs builds credibility and maturity. Carrying responsibility for everything else only creates unnecessary burden. Wisdom grows when leaders hold accountability without assuming blame.
- **Seek perspective from trusted counsel**
  Setbacks can narrow perspective and distort self-assessment. Trusted mentors, peers, and advisors provide clarity that is difficult to access alone. They help identify blind spots, affirm strengths, and challenge unhelpful narratives that leaders often carry in isolation. For Christian leaders, this may also include spiritual counsel, prayer, and Scripture. Growth rarely happens in isolation, and humility is often the doorway to renewed strength.
- **Apply lessons intentionally, not passively**
  Learning becomes growth only when it is applied. After reflection and counsel, leaders should intentionally identify how insights will shape future decisions, behaviors, or leadership approaches. This might involve refining communication, adjusting expectations, strengthening boundaries, or changing how risk is assessed. Growth is not about avoiding future setbacks altogether, but about responding with greater wisdom when they occur.

- **Care for your emotional and spiritual health**
  Leadership setbacks often take a quiet toll on emotional and spiritual well-being. Ignoring that toll can lead to burnout, discouragement, or cynicism. Christian leaders are called to steward not only their responsibilities, but also their hearts. Prayer, rest, community, and time for reflection are not luxuries. They are essential disciplines that sustain long-term leadership. Strength grows when leaders tend to their inner life with the same care they give to organizational demands.
- **Extend grace to yourself and to others**
  Finally, growth requires grace. Leaders who learn to extend grace to themselves are better equipped to extend grace to others who stumble, struggle, or fall short. This does not mean lowering standards or avoiding accountability. It means leading with compassion, patience, and understanding, shaped by the recognition that everyone is learning. Grace transforms setbacks into opportunities for shared growth rather than private shame.

Spiritual Resilience in Leadership

One of the most difficult disciplines in leadership is releasing outcomes that are ultimately beyond our control. For healthcare leaders trained to plan, analyze, and problem-solve, this can feel especially challenging. Yet faith offers something that professional skill alone cannot provide: perspective. Trusting God does not remove responsibility, but it does release the burden of believing that everything depends solely on us.

Scripture is filled with examples of faithful leaders who experienced repeated setbacks. Moses faced resistance, frustration, and long seasons where progress seemed slow or nonexistent. David endured failure, personal sin, betrayal, and prolonged uncertainty, even after being chosen as king. The apostle Paul encountered rejection, imprisonment, and hardship despite his obedience and calling. None of these leaders were defined by uninterrupted success. They were shaped by perseverance, repentance, and trust in God's purposes.

David's story is particularly instructive. He experienced both external opposition and internal failure, yet he consistently returned to God in humility and dependence. Instead of allowing setbacks to end his calling, he allowed them to refine his character. His resilience was not rooted in flawless leadership, but in a relationship with God that sustained him through disappointment and uncertainty.

For Christian healthcare leaders, spiritual resilience complements professional resilience. Faith provides a framework for meaning when outcomes fall short and hope when progress is slow. Prayer, Scripture, and trust in God's sovereignty enable leaders to carry responsibility without being weighed down by outcomes alone. In this way, faith does not replace professional competence, but strengthens it, helping leaders persevere with humility, wisdom, and grace.

Rising, Learning, and Leading

Setbacks are not the exception in leadership. They are part of the journey. While they rarely feel like a gift in the moment, growth is shaped by how leaders respond. For Christian healthcare leaders, the call is not to avoid failure, but to rise, learn, and continue serving with faithfulness and humility.

Leadership is not always easy. The weight of responsibility can feel heavy, and the path forward is often unclear. Yet we are not asked to carry that burden alone. Christ walks beside us in seasons of uncertainty, offering strength, wisdom, and grace when our own resources fall short. Setbacks do not mark the end of our calling. They are often the very means through which God shapes our character and equips us to lead with greater impact.

Action Step 1: Pause and Reflect

After a setback, take time to honestly assess what happened. Ask yourself what was within your control, what could have been done differently, and what lessons can guide your future decisions. Reflection should be constructive, not self-critical, and should focus on growth rather than blame.

Action Step 2: Seek Counsel and Perspective

Share the experience with a trusted mentor, peer, or spiritual advisor. Others can help you see blind spots, offer encouragement, and provide wisdom you may miss in the moment. Incorporate prayer or Scripture as a way to gain clarity and reassurance during this process.

Action Step 3: Apply Lessons Intentionally

Identify one or two specific changes you can make based on what you learned. This could involve adjusting leadership practices, improving communication, or refining decision-making processes. Commit to applying these lessons in your next steps rather than letting the setback define your future actions.

Action Step 4: Care for Your Heart and Extend Grace

Nurture your emotional, mental, and spiritual well-being. Take time for rest, reflection, and prayer. Practice self-compassion and remember that setbacks do not define your worth. Extending grace to yourself allows you to extend grace to others, fostering a culture of resilience and empathy in your leadership.

Reflection and Journal Prompts

1. Write about a recent situation where outcomes did not go as you hoped. How did you initially frame the experience, as a failure or a temporary setback? How did that framing impact your emotions, decisions, or actions?
2. Consider what this experience taught you about your leadership, decision-making, or approach to challenges. What insights could you apply to similar situations in the future? How might God be using this experience to shape your character or faith?
3. Reflect on what aspects of the situation were truly within your control, and what was influenced by external factors. How might letting go of what you cannot control change your perspective or reduce unnecessary stress in similar circumstances?
4. Based on this reflection, write down one or two concrete actions you can take to apply these lessons moving forward. How will you practice self-compassion and extend grace to yourself and others as you implement these changes?

Lesson 47

Live with Gratitude

Sometimes, it can be hard to feel grateful. The pressures, challenges, and complexity of healthcare are unrelenting. Yet one of the best things you can do for yourself and your team is to cultivate a mindset of gratitude. Gratitude is always a choice, and it has the power to shape both your life and your organization.

It is important to remember that ups and downs are normal. There will be difficult seasons as well as more stable ones. Even in the most challenging times, there are always things for which we can give thanks. It is striking that two people can face the same situation and respond very differently. One may recognize a difficult season as temporary and intentionally focus on the good in their life, thanking God for the blessings they have received. Another may lose sight of the joy that remains, allowing their focus to narrow until only frustration, fear, or disappointment dominates.

Yet what we focus on often grows in influence over time. For this reason, it is wise to direct your time, energy, and attention toward the gifts God has given you. At the same time, focus on your hopes, plans, and the ways you can use your strengths to serve others. Joy is not the absence of difficulty. It can be found even in the midst of it.

For Christian healthcare leaders, this perspective has a direct connection to our work. Challenges are common. Resources may feel insufficient. Pressures and expectations can be overwhelming. In these moments, how we respond matters. Our posture, whether marked by gratitude or discouragement, sets the tone for our teams and shapes organizational culture. It influences how colleagues experience their work and how

DOI: 10.4324/9781003769781-52

patients experience their care. When gratitude leads our hearts, it becomes visible in our leadership.

Gratitude Through the Lens of Faith

Scripture provides many reminders about gratitude and how we are meant to live as followers of Christ. One of the clearest is:

> Give thanks in all circumstances; for this is God's will for you in Christ Jesus.
>
> 1 Thessalonians 5:18 (NIV)

This verse reminds us that gratitude is not only for easy seasons. It is a deliberate, daily choice. Even in challenging moments, giving thanks shapes our perspective and aligns our hearts with God's will. Another passage emphasizes how gratitude can influence our peace and mindset:

> Do not be anxious about anything, but in every situation, by prayer and petition, with thanksgiving, present your requests to God. And the peace of God, which transcends all understanding, will guard your hearts and your minds in Christ Jesus.
>
> Philippians 4:6–7 (NIV)

This guidance is reassuring and timely for Christian healthcare leaders today. Anxiety often comes with the job, and the pressure can feel relentless. Yet we are instructed to bring our worries to God, along with gratitude for the blessings in our lives. In doing so, we open ourselves to His peace, which protects both our hearts and minds. Another passage highlights how gratitude can shape leadership and organizational culture:

> Let the peace of Christ rule in your hearts, since as members of one body you were called to peace. And be thankful. Let the message of Christ dwell among you richly as you teach and admonish one another with all wisdom through psalms, hymns, and songs from the Spirit, singing to God with gratitude in your hearts. And whatever you do, whether in word or deed, do it all in the name of the Lord Jesus, giving thanks to God the Father through him.
>
> Colossians 3:15–17 (NIV)

We are called to let our hearts and actions be guided by the peace of Christ and a spirit of thankfulness. When we do this, we are better equipped to lead others in Christ's name, demonstrating gratitude in both word and deed.

How Gratitude Shapes Culture

Many of us have worked for leaders who are genuinely grateful for their roles, their teams, and their organizations. That gratitude shows in how they show up each day, treat others, and speak about their work. It often extends beyond the workplace as well. You may hear them speak appreciatively about their families or notice the joy they find in activities outside of work. This broader posture of gratitude gives their leadership authenticity and depth.

Perhaps most powerful is how these leaders respond during difficult times. Rather than dwelling on what is broken or beyond their control, they focus on what constructive work can still be done. They recognize challenges clearly, yet reframe them in ways that invite learning, collaboration, and hope. In doing so, they help others remain grounded and forward-looking, even in uncertain circumstances.

If these are the leaders we long to work for, it serves us well to model this same posture ourselves. Our personal example is one of our most influential tools, and gratitude shapes organizational culture in tangible, intentional ways. Leaders can weave gratitude into the life of their teams and organizations through specific practices, including those below.

- **Model appreciative leadership**
  Leaders who regularly express gratitude, both publicly and privately, set a tone of respect and humility. Noticing effort, faithfulness, and progress signals to others that their contributions matter.
- **Recognize people consistently, not just outcomes**
  Gratitude shifts recognition beyond results to include character, teamwork, growth, and perseverance. This encourages engagement and reinforces values, not just performance.
- **Shape everyday language and conversations**
  Grateful leaders are intentional about how they speak, focusing on possibilities rather than problems, and on progress rather than perfection. Over time, this language influences how teams discuss challenges and approach their work.

- **Respond to challenges with perspective and hope**
  When difficulties arise, leaders grounded in gratitude acknowledge reality without becoming consumed by it. They help teams see what can still be done and where God is at work, even in uncertainty.
- **Create space for reflection and celebration**
  Gratitude grows when leaders intentionally pause to reflect on milestones, lessons learned, and shared successes. These moments strengthen connection, resilience, and a sense of shared purpose.
- **Encourage service-centered leadership**
  A grateful posture reminds leaders that their role is ultimately one of stewardship. This fosters a culture where service, compassion, and care for others are prioritized.

How Gratitude Leads to Peace

Focusing on gratitude is not about being overly optimistic or naïve. It is about accepting the present moment as it is, while intentionally recognizing all that we have to be thankful for. This is a grounded, faith-based approach to living and one of the most effective ways to cultivate mindfulness and inner peace.

As Christians, we see this guidance woven throughout Scripture. Practicing gratitude has the power to transform not only our perspective but our daily actions. Beyond its personal benefits, living with thankfulness serves as a visible witness to our relationship with Jesus Christ. In a world where gratitude is increasingly rare, choosing to lead with a grateful heart sets us apart. It shapes how we respond to challenges, how we treat our teams, and how we influence the culture around us.

Ultimately, a heart rooted in gratitude opens the door to peace, joy, and resilience. Even in difficult seasons, it reminds us that God's presence and provision remain. This assurance equips us to lead with hope, humility, and purpose.

Action Step 1: Begin Each Day with Intentional Gratitude

Start your day by naming three things you are grateful for, personally, professionally, or spiritually. Offer them to God in prayer, asking Him to shape your perspective before the pressures of the day take hold.

Action Step 2: Practice Visible Gratitude in Your Leadership

Make it a habit to regularly thank team members for their effort, faithfulness, and character, not just results. Be specific and sincere, whether in private conversations or public settings.

Action Step 3: Reframe Challenges Through a Gratitude Lens

When difficulties arise, acknowledge them honestly, and then intentionally ask: *What remains good here? What can we still do? Where might God be at work?* Use this framing to guide team conversations and decisions.

Action Step 4: Create Rhythms of Reflection and Celebration

Set aside intentional time on a regular basis (for example, a few minutes at the start of weekly meetings or at the end of major projects) to reflect on what went well, lessons learned, and signs of progress. Use this time to express thanks, to God and to one another, so gratitude becomes a consistent and visible part of your team's rhythm, not an afterthought.

Reflection and Journal Prompts

1. Reflect on the areas of your life or leadership where your attention most often goes. Are you more focused on what is lacking or on what God has already provided? How might intentionally shifting your focus change your outlook and responses?
2. Consider how your attitude, whether marked by gratitude or discouragement, shows up in your words, decisions, and interactions. How might your posture be shaping the culture of your team or organization?
3. Identify a current challenge you are facing. What sources of gratitude still exist within or alongside that difficulty? How can recognizing these blessings help you lead with greater peace and hope?
4. Reflect on how gratitude shows up in your prayer life and daily leadership practices. In what ways could you more intentionally give thanks to God in all circumstances, trusting Him even when outcomes are uncertain?

Lesson 48

Celebrate Successes

One thing we do not do enough of in healthcare organizations is celebrate successes. Too often, only large achievements are recognized, and even then, not well. In addition, we tend to celebrate only one kind of success, usually defined by business outcomes. Yet what we choose to celebrate sends a powerful message throughout the organization. Those actions are more likely to be repeated, and they clearly signal what we value. For Christian healthcare leaders, this deserves thoughtful and intentional consideration.

You rarely hear someone say they celebrate too much at work. Imagine hearing, "Oh yes, they are always celebrating our success. I am really tired of it." That sounds almost absurd. In the same way, most people do not complain that they are thanked too often for their hard work. Celebration and gratitude go hand in hand. Both communicate appreciation, but celebration goes a step further by bringing people together.

If you want to build a true team, there must be shared purpose, mutual respect, support, encouragement, and above all, trust. Yet trust alone is not enough. People also need a sense of meaning. They need to feel they are working toward something that matters, not simply enduring another day to keep the wheels turning. Unfortunately, this is the reality in many healthcare roles and organizations.

I have experienced both kinds of environments in my career, and perhaps you have as well. It is possible to feel truly alive and energized by the impact of your work in healthcare. When you are part of meaningful change and regularly pause to celebrate the significance of that work, it changes everything. On the other hand, when each day feels like another

DOI: 10.4324/9781003769781-53

crisis to manage or another change initiative to survive, discouragement can quickly take root.

The key is deciding in advance what you value, what you will celebrate, how often you will do it, and how you will do it. This may sound contrived, but without intentional planning, it is easy to be overwhelmed by the relentless pace of organizational life. A culture of celebration does not happen by accident. It is a deliberate and meaningful choice.

The Joy That Sustains

In the book of Nehemiah, God's people returned to Jerusalem after years of exile. The city lay in ruins, and rebuilding the wall was difficult, exhausting, and often discouraging work. Yet through perseverance and God's faithfulness, the wall was completed.

When the work ended, the people gathered to hear God's Word. Instead of pushing them immediately toward the next task, Nehemiah and the other leaders gave a surprising instruction:

> Do not grieve, for the joy of the Lord is your strength.
>
> Nehemiah 8:10 (NIV)

They invited the people to pause, celebrate, and rejoice together.

This moment reminds us that celebration is not merely a reward for hard work. It is a source of renewal. The people needed joy as much as they needed guidance. By intentionally creating space to celebrate, their leaders restored strength, unity, and hope for what lay ahead.

In healthcare leadership, the work can feel unending, and pausing may seem impractical when needs continue to press in. Yet Scripture shows us that joy is sustaining, not indulgent. When leaders choose to celebrate progress, express gratitude, and rejoice together, they help others remember the meaning and impact of their work and draw strength for the road ahead.

Choosing What to Celebrate

What we choose to celebrate is just as important as celebrating itself. As noted earlier, recognition should not be limited to only grand achievements, nor should it focus solely on business metrics. It is equally vital to notice and honor everyday efforts, acts of service, and small wins that reflect dedication, teamwork, and the values we hold as leaders. Examples include:

- A team member going above and beyond to support a colleague or patient
- Small improvements in workflow or patient care that make a difference
- Acts of kindness, compassion, or encouragement within the team
- Milestones in professional development or skill-building
- Creative solutions that solve persistent problems
- Moments when the team demonstrates core values in action

Celebration is more than a simple recognition or shout-out. It requires intentionally slowing down to bond and rejoice with your team. There are many ways to do this, but it must be genuine. Rushed, superficial, or token celebrations are quickly noticed by teams and can be counterproductive.

The Benefits of Celebrations

Creating a culture of celebration isn't just beneficial for teams. It benefits senior leaders as well. Leadership can be isolating, and intentionally creating opportunities for positive social interaction makes the work more sustainable. Often, we don't realize how much we need these moments until we pause and slow down. Celebration allows us to feel human again and see each other beyond organizational roles.

These are the moments when people let down their guards, laugh, and relax. Teams that celebrate together tend to stay together, while teams without healthy personal connections often struggle to remain cohesive. Celebration isn't a distraction from work. It is a vital part of building trust, resilience, and lasting engagement. Over time, it fosters a positive organizational culture grounded in encouragement and connection.

The Importance of Joy

As Christian healthcare leaders, we have an opportunity to restore a sense of joy to those around us. If we surveyed healthcare leaders and professionals across a typical organization, how many would say they regularly experience joy in their work? Likely not many, but it is possible. Ultimately, it comes down to leadership.

There is a saying that people don't leave jobs. They leave supervisors. A leader can make a significant difference in the quality of life, satisfaction, and joy experienced by their team. While we cannot control all the pressures, constraints, and flaws of our healthcare system, we can choose small, concrete actions that help people rise above them. Celebration, gratitude, and encouragement are examples of this.

The good news is that cultivating joy isn't complicated. It simply requires intention. Here are a few practical ways this can be done in a healthcare setting:

- Take a moment to thank individuals or teams for specific acts of service
- Celebrate small wins, not just major achievements
- Create brief, intentional moments of connection such as morning huddles, team check-ins, or shared reflections
- Encourage laughter and lighthearted interactions where appropriate
- Recognize and honor the unique strengths and contributions of each team member
- Offer opportunities for team members to support each other and celebrate shared successes

This list is not comprehensive, but it provides a starting point for fostering healthier teams and cultures. When we reflect on what it means to be a Christian healthcare leader, this can be a defining distinction: if we feel the joy of Christ in our own hearts, we have an opportunity to extend it to others. Once we understand this, it becomes a matter of simply letting our light shine, especially in difficult seasons. Even a small act of joy can be like a breath of fresh air to those who are struggling.

Leadership isn't only about achieving results. It's also about recognizing and celebrating others along the way. Doing so supports your team, builds morale, and reinforces a culture of collaboration and excellence. It inspires continued growth and leaves a lasting legacy of encouragement and affirmation.

Action Step 1: Identify What to Celebrate

Decide in advance which achievements, behaviors, or milestones matter most to you and your team. Include not just grand outcomes, but small wins, acts of service, creativity, and evidence of your organization's core values.

Action Step 2: Schedule Intentional Celebration

Make celebration a deliberate part of your calendar. Pause during busy seasons to acknowledge progress, rather than waiting for "perfect" outcomes.

Action Step 3: Express Gratitude and Recognition Personally

Thank individuals and teams for specific contributions, both publicly and privately. Combine verbal recognition with tangible actions such as notes, small celebrations, or opportunities for shared joy.

Action Step 4: Foster a Culture of Joy and Connection

Encourage moments of laughter, lighthearted interactions, and meaningful connection across roles. Model celebrating others' successes yourself, helping your team see that joy and appreciation are part of everyday leadership.

Reflection and Journal Prompts

1. What types of achievements or behaviors do I naturally notice and celebrate in my team? Are there small wins, acts of service, or moments of alignment with core values that I overlook?
2. How often do I intentionally pause to recognize or celebrate progress in my organization? What might be preventing me from doing this more regularly?
3. How do my words and actions of recognition affect team morale, trust, and engagement? Can I recall a moment when celebrating someone or something positively changed the team's energy or motivation?
4. What concrete steps can I take in the next week or month to celebrate successes more intentionally? How can I model joy, gratitude, and recognition in a way that aligns with my Christian leadership values?

Lesson 49

Finish Faithfully

As you reflect on your journey, it is natural to think about the things you might have done differently. Yet the most important thing is not how you start, but how you finish. This is especially true as you come to the end of a book like this one. There are many ways to reflect the heart of Christ in a hurting world, and often it is only through reflection that we begin to see how we can live and lead differently.

It can be tempting to be hard on yourself, replaying situations where you did not live up to these ideals. But this, too, is part of being human. What matters most is not past perfection, but how you choose to approach each new day.

The good news is that meaningful change does not require grand gestures or dramatic overhauls. The most lasting transformation happens through small, consistent actions practiced over time. You do not have to apply every lesson in this book, and you do not have to apply them perfectly or all at once. But the more consistently you practice them in the moments that matter, the more likely it is that something new will take shape in the lives of those around you. In doing so, you will not only transform the culture of your organization but also yourself.

Building New Habits

Many of the lessons in this book involve breaking old habits and patterns, including ingrained ways of thinking and acting. They also require building new ones. This kind of change rarely happens overnight. It takes time,

DOI: 10.4324/9781003769781-54

repetition, and intentional practice for new pathways to form. At first, these changes require conscious effort, but over time they become more natural and automatic. This process requires discipline, humility, resilience in the face of setbacks, and a deep commitment to growth.

The result is a leader who is strong, steady, and trustworthy, the kind others often assume was born with Christlike character. You now know that this kind of leadership is not accidental. It is cultivated. It takes intention and concrete steps to embed these principles into your life and into the fabric of your organization.

Beginning a New Journey

This book is not meant to be all-encompassing. It is meant to begin a journey. There are many ways to go beyond the lessons offered here. Think of them as a spark, an invitation to consciously reflect on what it truly means to be a Christian healthcare leader. That was the central question my editor asked when I first proposed this book: "What do you mean by a Christian healthcare leader?" If so many people are drawn to healthcare out of a desire to help others, is there really a difference?

This book offers an opportunity to explore that question personally, and it begins within you. What does it mean for you to serve as a Christian healthcare leader? How should it guide the way you form others, build teams, and shape organizations? What are you being called to do, and what legacy do you hope to leave?

Reflecting on Finishing Faithfully

Finishing faithfully applies to both your work and your life. Regardless of where you are on your journey, this lesson invites you to reflect on both:

- **Look back with honesty and grace**
  Where have you seen growth in your leadership over time? Where do you still notice resistance, old habits, or unfinished work?
- **Define what "finishing faithfully" means to you**
  How do you define faithfulness at this stage of your life and career, not in theory, but in daily practice?

- **Identify the small practices that matter most**
  Which one or two lessons from this book feel most important for you to continue living out consistently?
- **Consider your influence on others**
  How do your choices, reactions, and priorities shape the culture of your team or organization?
- **Assess resilience and perseverance**
  When you fall short, how do you typically respond? What would it look like to get back up with humility and resolve?
- **Name the legacy you are building**
  If someone were to describe your leadership years from now, what qualities would you hope they would name?
- **Commit to a next step**
  What is one concrete action you can take in the coming weeks to continue leading with intention and faithfulness?

Taking the First Steps Toward a New Future

Some of you may use this moment to reflect on what it means to live as a Christian in every aspect of your life. You may find yourself reflecting not only on your calling within healthcare, but on your broader calling altogether. Where is God leading you now? Seasons change, and so do callings. God often calls people to serve faithfully in one setting and then, in time, to step into another.

It is also a chance to reflect on how God has walked with you so far, through your decisions, lessons learned, and the priorities that have shaped your journey. As you may already recognize, the principles in this book are not limited to healthcare or leadership roles. They apply across vocations, relationships, and life beyond work. My hope is that you will continue to reflect on them and allow them to guide you wherever your path leads. As you take the first steps into a new chapter, you can do so with confidence. Scripture reminds us that we do not walk alone:

> Being confident of this, that he who began a good work in you will carry it on to completion until the day of Christ Jesus.
>
> Philippians 1:6 (NIV)

Faithful leadership, and faithful living, is not about perfection, but perseverance. Like the apostle Paul, our aim is simply to be able to say in the end:

> I have fought the good fight, I have finished the race, I have kept the faith.
>
> 2 Timothy 4:7 (NIV)

A Final Word

If this book leaves you with one invitation, it is this: remain faithful to the work God has placed before you today, trusting Him with what lies ahead. You may not always see the full impact of your leadership, your choices, or your quiet acts of integrity, but God does. As you continue your journey, may you lead with courage, humility, and compassion, anchored in faith and guided by hope. And when your season of leadership is complete, may you look back with gratitude, knowing you did not strive for perfection, but chose, day by day, to finish faithfully.

Action Step 1: Choose One Practice to Carry Forward

Identify a single habit, mindset, or leadership practice from this book that you will intentionally continue over the next season. Write it down and define what faithfulness to it looks like in your daily life.

Action Step 2: Build Reflection into Your Routine

Set aside regular time, weekly or monthly, to reflect on your leadership, decisions, and priorities. Use this time to honestly assess where you are growing and where you may need to realign with your values.

Action Step 3: Anchor Your Leadership in Scripture and Prayer

Commit to grounding your leadership decisions in prayer and Scripture. Even brief, consistent moments of spiritual grounding can shape how you respond under pressure and lead with integrity.

Action Step 4: Lead with Intention in the Moments That Matter Most

Pay attention to everyday interactions, including conversations, decisions, and reactions, especially during challenging moments. Choose to lead with humility, compassion, and faithfulness, knowing that small, consistent actions shape lasting culture.

Reflection and Journal Prompts

1. Reflect on your leadership journey so far. What are three specific ways you have grown, and where do you still notice patterns or habits that hold you back? How can you respond to these areas with both honesty and grace?
2. What does "finishing faithfully" mean to you in your current season of life and work? How can this definition guide the way you make daily choices, interact with others, and approach challenges?
3. Identify one or two key habits or practices from this book that you want to carry forward. How will you intentionally embed them into your daily routine, and what signs will indicate that they are becoming a natural part of your leadership?
4. Imagine someone describing your leadership years from now. What qualities or impacts would you hope they highlight? How can the choices you make this week help you move closer to that legacy?

Lesson 50

Let God Write the Final Chapter

Sometimes the hardest thing in life is to surrender to God and trust Him to accomplish what we cannot. But as Christian healthcare leaders, this is exactly what we are called to do. After doing our best to act faithfully, we must entrust our leadership, influence, and legacy to God. As Proverbs reminds us:

> Commit to the Lord whatever you do, and he will establish your plans.
>
> Proverbs 16:3 (NIV)

This principle is essential in both our work and personal lives. Many circumstances are beyond our control, and learning to release the outcome to God is a vital part of living in faith. It also offers the promise of deep inner peace, which is crucial amid the pressures and complexity of healthcare.

A Story of Surrender

In my own leadership journey, I came to a place of surrender, but only after reaching my limits. I have always been driven and committed to high standards. Yet in retrospect, I sometimes relied more on myself than

DOI: 10.4324/9781003769781-55

on God, pursuing knowledge, development, and best practices through mentors and leadership opportunities.

But even the best preparation cannot solve every problem an organization faces. In one particularly challenging organization, I reached the limits of what I could accomplish on my own. When my efforts were exhausted, I turned to God. I didn't receive immediate solutions, but I did receive the strength to continue serving and uphold our mission. At the same time, God opened doors to new opportunities where my abilities could grow and be used more fully.

Some of these opportunities were extraordinary, but I didn't act immediately. I stayed rooted in fear, including fear of change, the unknown, and losing the comfort of my previous position. Ultimately, I did take action, but not before my physical, mental, and spiritual health had been strained. This doesn't have to happen to you.

Letting God write the final chapter means trusting Him in your current situation while remaining attentive to the opportunities He places before you. Surrendering is not just turning over your anxieties. It is also opening your eyes to how God is leading.

Turning the Page

Letting God write the final chapter doesn't mean the story is over. It simply means a new page is being turned. This may continue within your current organization, or it may lead you somewhere new. The most important thing to remember is that God is walking beside you. He will never leave or forsake you. That is the promise of a relationship with God through Jesus Christ.

Visualize it this way: you are on a pathway winding through a valley. The sun has set, and the world has grown dim. You can see the path ahead only faintly. Yet, you are not alone. Someone walks beside you, your faithful companion, already familiar with the path ahead. When you notice Him, any fear fades. A reassuring hand rests on your shoulder, accompanied by a comforting smile and nod, and you feel a deep peace knowing He is guiding your journey.

Implications for Healthcare Leadership

For healthcare leaders, this means leading with humility and trust rather than trying to control every outcome. It means modeling faith, composure, and resilience under pressure for your team. Most importantly, it means recognizing that your influence is greatest when you allow God to guide the final outcomes. These principles can first be internalized personally, then incorporated into the formation of others, and ultimately woven into organizational culture. As Christian healthcare leaders, the ultimate lesson is this: our best work comes when we faithfully do our part and trust God to write the final chapter.

A Closing Reflection

The story of your leadership, and of your life, is still being written. Each day is a new page. Each decision a new line. Your work matters, your influence matters, and so does your faith. Yet the true author of the story is God. When you surrender to Him, you are not giving up. You are gaining clarity, peace, and purpose. You are allowing your leadership, your service, and your life to align with His greater plan. Step forward with courage, serve with faith, and rest knowing that the final chapter is in His hands. And what He is writing is far greater than anything you could imagine.

Action Step 1: Identify Areas of Control to Release

Make a list of decisions, projects, or situations where you feel the need to control the outcome. Pray over each item, consciously handing it over to God and trusting Him to guide the results.

Action Step 2: Create a Daily Surrender Practice

Set aside a few minutes each day to pause, pray, and reaffirm your trust in God. Use a short phrase like: *"Lord, I surrender this to You. Guide my steps and my influence today."*

Action Step 3: Stay Alert to Opened Doors

Keep a journal of opportunities or nudges from God, whether in your current work, community, or personal life. Reflect weekly on where He may be guiding you and what actions you can take in faith.

Action Step 4: Model Faith and Trust for Your Team

When challenges arise, demonstrate calm, humility, and reliance on God rather than stress or micromanagement. Share lessons from your own journey of surrender, helping others see that trusting God is both practical and transformative.

Reflection and Journal Prompts

1. What situations, decisions, or outcomes in your work or life do you feel the need to control? How might your perspective or peace change if you intentionally release these to God?
2. Recall a time when you tried to solve a problem on your own. What was the outcome? How might your approach have been different if you had fully trusted God to guide the process?
3. Are there doors or opportunities in your life that you've noticed but hesitated to act on? What might God be inviting you to explore if you act in faith rather than fear?
4. How do your responses under pressure reflect your trust in God? What steps can you take to demonstrate faith and calm to your team or those you lead, so they can see trust in action?

Epilogue

As we close this book, I want to acknowledge the weight of healthcare leadership. I know the exhaustion, doubt, and quiet faithfulness many of you carry. This work is demanding, often unseen, and rarely simple, yet it matters deeply. You are not alone, and the choices you make, the care you offer, and the integrity you uphold ripple far beyond what you can see.

Leadership is not about fixing every problem or controlling every outcome. It is about showing up faithfully, trusting God to work through your decisions, and allowing Him to shape the ultimate story. The quiet acts of service, the ethical choices no one notices, and the instances of compassion that cost time or energy are the moments that define culture and leave lasting impact.

There will be seasons of doubt, discouragement, and frustration. That is part of the journey. What matters most is remaining rooted in faith, letting it guide your words, your actions, and your presence. Lead with courage, listen with humility, and extend the same grace to yourself that you offer so freely to others.

Your leadership, your influence, and your life are still being written. God is the true author of this story, and when you surrender to Him, you gain clarity, peace, and purpose. Step forward with confidence, serve with integrity, and remain present in every moment. And as your story unfolds, remember that God is at work not only through your successes but also through your perseverance, your questions, and even your limitations. May you continue to lead faithfully, love generously, and trust deeply. The final chapter is in His hands, and you can walk forward in trust, knowing He is already at work in ways you cannot yet see.

Index

For Product Safety Concerns and Information please contact our EU
representative GPSR@taylorandfrancis.com
Taylor & Francis Verlag GmbH, Kaufingerstraße 24, 80331 München, Germany

www.ingramcontent.com/pod-product-compliance
Lightning Source LLC
LaVergne TN
LVHW060805080826
845179LV00036B/323
* 9 7 8 1 0 4 1 2 9 4 8 4 9 *